THE MURDERING OF MY YEARS

ARTISTS & ACTIVISTS MAKING ENDS MEET

BY MICKEY Z.

SOFT SKILL BOOKS, BROOKLYN, NY 2003

THE MURDERING OF MY YEARS:
ARTISTS AND ACTIVISTS MAKING ENDS MEETS

ISBN: 1-887128-78-6
©COPYRIGHT 2003 BY MICKEY Z.

FIRST EDITION

PRINTED IN CANADA BY KROMAR PRINTING LTD.

BOOK DESIGN: DAVID JANIK

DISTRIBUTED BY PUBLISHERS GROUP WEST
WWW.PGW.COM | TEL. 800 788 3123

SOFT SKILL BOOKS

AN IMPRINT OF

SOFT SKULL PRESS
71 BOND STREET
BROOKLYN, NY 11217
WWW.SOFTSKULL.COM

ACKNOWLEDGEMENTS

Of course, I want to first thank all the participants in this book for making time to answer my questions and for following through on a commitment.

Thanks to *everyone* at Soft Skull Press (past and present). I owe you all so much. Special thanks to Richard Nash for his enthusiasm for this project and David Janik for the hard work he put into it.

I'd like to voice my respect and appreciation and affection for my agent, Claudia Menza.

Thank you to my family, friends, colleagues, and all those who—whether or not they even realized it—have played a role in inspiring and/or facilitating my artistic and activist evolution.

To all my bosses and supervisors and co-workers over the years, well, I hope you know how I feel about you.

Since this book was done almost entirely via e-mail, I'd like to acknowledge Jeff Pabon for hooking me up with a free computer a few years back and getting me started on the Internet.

Thank you to the Puffin Foundation for the generous writing grant that helped make this book possible.

To Hank: for the title and the inspiration.

Finally, to artists and activists everywhere—especially those who toil under conditions I hope to never experience—I declare my undying gratitude, admiration, and solidarity.

I always resented all the years, the hours, the minutes I gave them as a working stiff. It actually hurt my head, my insides, it made me dizzy and a bit crazy. I couldn't understand the murdering of my years.
—CHARLES BUKOWSKI

I've never had any shitty jobs.
—KATE MOSS

To Michele
You not only make it possible for me to do what I do,
you make it all worthwhile

TABLE OF CONTENTS

CONTENTS (CON'T)

CONTENTS (CON'T)

AUTHOR'S PREFACE

NEVER HEARD FROM AGAIN?

The rewards for playing ball with the system in this society and this culture are very clear. The financial rewards are obvious. What about the other side of the coin? What about the punishments?
—DAVID BARSAMIAN

Societies differ. It can happen [in the U.S.], but it's not on the scale of a state that really terrorizes its own citizens. If you come from the more privileged classes, if you're a white middle-class person, then the chances that you are going to be subjected to literal state terror are very slight. It could happen, but it's slight. What will happen is that you'll be marginalized, excluded. Instead of becoming part of the privileged elite, you'll be driving a taxi cab. It's not torture, but very few people are going to select that option, if they have a choice. And the ones who do select it will never be heard from again. Therefore they are not part of the indoctrination system. They don't make it. It could be worse, but it's enough to discipline people.
—NOAM CHOMSKY

Sooner or later (as Ani DiFranco reminds us in her poem, "My IQ") every school child encounters a test in which they are shown, say, two squares and a circle. The Q&A that inevitably accompanies these images will go like this:

Q. Which one doesn't belong?
A. The circle.

Consequently, at the tender age of 5 or 6, we are taught that different does not belong. The 24 individuals who have shared their stories in this book just might have been absent on the day that exam was administered. Each of them has made the premeditated decision to become an activist and/or artist and, by definition, be "different" in a culture that values sameness while marginalizing individuality.

As Professor Chomsky articulates above, the price paid for being different in other nations is considerably higher than that in the U.S., and this book is *not* a collection of stories from whiny, misunderstood geniuses blaming the world for their perceived misfortune. Rather, *The Murdering of My Years* offers a sampling from a nearly invisible minority in this coast-to-coast mall we call America. Activists engage in social action during their "free time" with no promise of results (other than police harassment and societal stigma). Artists create—often without even a glimmer of possibility that financial remuneration lurks anywhere on the horizon. Such acts, I submit, are revolutionary within the context of a corporate capitalist social order.

Everywhere we are inundated with the American theology of individualism within the entrepreneur model. The "heroes" that are packaged and sold to us are Wall Street speculators, professional athletes, and digitally- or surgically-enhanced celebrities. The dreams we are encouraged to fulfill seem to be limited to appearing on television, purchasing consumer electronics, and gambling on the lottery. Civil society is vanishing while fortitude is measured by bungee jumps, morality is dropped along with cluster bombs from 15,000 feet, and solidarity has been reduced to waiting on line for hours to see a blockbuster film.

The participants in this book (myself included) aren't martyrs or heroes. Artists and activists are driven by more than material accumulation and, as a result, are often relegated to the margins. *The Murdering of My Years* is one small step toward widening those margins and making "different" belong.

EARN WITHOUT SELLING OUT?

Twenty years of schooling and they put you on the day shift.
—BOB DYLAN

There were two converging catalysts in the writing of this book. In 2001, I finally got around to reading Frank McCourt's best selling memoir, *Angela's Ashes*, and found myself captivated. This got me thinking about the notion of memoirs in general. Sure, McCourt grew up in abject poverty but most humans on the planet today dwell in abject poverty. McCourt's life story is far from exceptional.

    Q. What made Frank McCourt's autobiography special?
    A. The way it was told.

    Well, I thought to myself: *My life has been at least as interesting as Frank McCourt's. Why don't I pen a memoir?* I commenced making notes and working up the nerve to share this scheme with my agent.

    Meanwhile, back in Astoria, running parallel to my memoir fixation, more money was needed in the Zezima household. My wife, Michele, works as a pediatric physical therapist. As the job title implies, the work is *physical*. There was no way around it. She needed more help from me on the fiscal end of things. But how would I earn without selling out and still have time to write?

    To help answer that, I e-mailed several colleagues to see how they were managing. As I read their replies, I grew fascinated with the results of this impromptu survey. If you had happened to be in the one-bedroom apartment Michele and I call home, you might have witnessed the image of a light bulb illuminating just above my shaved dome.

    What if I compiled a book based on this subject and included my own story as a provisional fix for my memoir mania? In short order, I amassed a list of potential suspects, wrote a concise e-mail invitation, and hit "send."

WORKING WITHOUT A NET

Uh, can anybody help out a young, poor, sad, poor, young, struggling musician?
I'm, uh, not hungry or anything, but I do have a huge phone bill.
—NYC SUBWAY MUSICIAN

The initial response to my e-mail varied widely. Some expressed genuine alarm at
the prospect of discussing how they made ends meet. For example:

"I try to sail beneath the radar on such matters."

"I wouldn't want to put on public record some of my survival techniques,
especially in the current political atmosphere, which is going to last a long time."

A particularly gratifying bit of feedback was from the many respondents
who saw it through to the end and found themselves enriched by this exercise in
self-examination.

In many cases, however, the response was no response at all. Well over 100
artists and activists were invited to participate and the vast majority did not even
acknowledge receiving the invitation. There were some who voiced interest but
employed the "I'm too busy" defense. Even more requested the questionnaire and
then promptly vanished. Others waited until they were reminded about the deadline to back out; some waited even longer. I wondered if this pattern was verifi-
cation of my thesis that the work of artists and activists is so de-valued in a cor-
porate-dominated society that few even have time to promote their efforts or
causes in a book. Then again, the remarkable lack of follow-through and the
sheer inability to hit a deadline may also speak to the type of people drawn to
non-mainstream pursuits and their unwitting complicity in the sad state of
things. (Either way, don't blame me for the disproportionate amount and vegetarians in this book. I invited a broad, nationwide cross-section of candidates.)

None of the above responses surprised me, but the number of those who
wondered why they were asked took me aback. They were, by their own admis-
sion, "doing nothing special" or "not really an activist" or merely "boring." That

last comment carried through to the answering of the questions I eventually proposed. Quite a few respondents apologized in advance for their "dull" lives and "mundane" answers. While this internalization of conventional perceptions is yet another obstacle lying in the path of any non-conformist, I'm here to declare that "dull" (as defined by today's one-size-fits-all society) is nothing to be ashamed of.

No one in *The Murdering of My Years* has climbed Mount Everest or won an Academy Award or appeared on a game show (at least that I know of). But their stories are authentic: no laugh track, nothing re-touched by computer software, very little editing on my part. These people are working without a net to create and/or disseminate art and dissenting opinions within a commercial framework designed to co-opt such output and feed it back to us as "trends." They are challenging the status quo. They are living their lives outside the cookie cutter formula.

Is the life of an unknown artist and/or activist dull or mundane? With so few mechanisms set up to facilitate such work, sure, it can be at times. However, I believe a more pertinent question remains:

Q. Are the struggles of artists and activists worth reading and sharing and emulating?
A. After reading the stories herein, I trust you'll agree they are.

With *The Murdering of My Years*, I hope to reveal an alternative paradigm by tapping into the motivating power of example. Beyond that, it's up to each individual reader to decide of what use these examples are.

As Mao urged: *Absorb what is useful; reject what is useless.*

As Bruce Lee modified: *Absorb what is useful and develop from there; add specifically what is your own.*

All paid jobs degrade and absorb the mind.
—ARISTOTLE

PARTICIPANT BIOGRAPHIES

JEN ANGEL (born: 1975): I currently live in Bowling Green, Ohio. I've been involved in zines and independent publishing for about 10 years. Right now I am publishing *Clamor* magazine with my partner, Jason Kucsma—it is a bimonthly, nationally distributed magazine about culture, politics, and media. I also publish an anthology of small press writing, and help put on the annual Underground Publishing Conference. During the day, I work at Planned Parenthood of Northwest Ohio, which helps support myself and Jason while we work on other projects. I have a degree in Political Science/Journalism from the Ohio State University. Besides Ohio, I lived in California for two years while I worked as coordinator for *MaximumRockNRoll*.

SETH ASHER (born: 1962): Four years ago marks the beginning of a dramatically transformational period for me. The seemingly pivotal event was my divorce and consequent reclaiming of critical thinking and independent action. What followed was a personal revolution: new community affiliations leading to new friends and acquaintances; a new home, food choices, transportation mode, and choice of clothing and home furnishings; a revamping of my personal politics, lifestyle, work-style, and career. There were all sorts of new patterns of living to learn and craft: bicycling for commuting, urban exploration and travel, Community Supported Agriculture work, Park Slope Food Coop work, community gardening, vegetarian food progressing to vegan food/lifestyle to the raw-food-vegan diet, browsing at and holding stoop sales. The neighborhood tailor altered my clothes to a new fit brought about by good food and yoga. This helped me to stop shopping at corporate giants with overseas slave wage operations such as Macy's, the Gap, and Banana Republic. Yoga, a healthful diet, and stress avoidance eventually replaced medical insurance; coconuts and other special fruit replaced restaurant expenses; active experiential participation replaced passive entertainment and other forms of indolence. Connecting with friends and belonging to my community replaced consuming. Learning replaced buying. Living simply replaced working for the shitty, wretched system. My bike replaced my car. At some point in this revolution, I felt secure enough to ditch my practice as a financial advisor and ultimately become a massage therapist. All of these changes are deeply inter-related; one facilitating the other. For instance, rejecting the automobile and attaining emotional and physical health were some steps instrumental in lessen-ing my financial burden that ultimately allowed me to stop working for the cor-porate machine. Monthly community raw-vegan potlucks, bike club rides and trips, free-for-volunteers classes and tours at the Brooklyn Botanic Garden, var-ied schedule of yoga classes, regular massage--these types of activities bring enough fun into my routine that financially and ecologically costly activities, like frequent plane travel for vacation 'escapes', are no longer needed.

GARY BADDELEY (born: 1965): I was born in London and was subjected to the best that British private education had to offer (quite a bit, as it turned out, not that I appreciated it at the time). I moved to New York in 1987 and have lived here since then. I told Mickey that I actually am mainstream, but he wouldn't listen. I think you'll agree with me once I list my activities in New York: Law degree from New York University; entertainment law practice acting for such diverse clients as Led Zeppelin and Nipper, the RCA dog; General Manager of Robbins Entertainment, a record label that legendary indie record man Cory Robbins started with BMG Entertainment; co-founder of The Disinformation Company Ltd. The last bit is non-mainstream, I guess: we put out some pretty subversive TV programs, books, websites and even a huge conference at the turn of the Millennium. It's also when I stopped working for someone else (which has its downside, as you shall see).

(Because of the nature of her work in the pro-choice movement, Rachel asked that we not publish her last name.)
RACHEL F. (born: 1965): Today my flexible work hours allow me to be involved with many wonderful groups. I'm on the steering committee of the Brooklyn ProChoice Network a volunteer clinic escort, and I host women who travel to NYC for abortions unavailable in their states. I serve on the coordinating com-mittee of my Green Party local chapter, and run a Green public speaking club.

4

I'm a volunteer compost educator at the local botanic gardens, and I'm certified with the Parks Department to voluntarily prune and maintain city street trees. I've been secretary, treasurer, and president of my 40-unit self-managed cooperative apartment building, and assist my Community Supported (organic) Agriculture cooperative buying club.

GEORGIA GIANNIKOURIS (born: 1981): I was born and raised in Astoria, NY. I currently live in New Milford, NJ, (I'm not entirely happy about that, but it's where I am), and I am a student at Fordham University. Besides that, I am a middle child, a dreamer, an idealist, an optimist, a lover of the arts, a black sheep, a philanthropist, a humanist, a peace-making attempter, and a believer. And I am much more than that. I create my own world, and it brings me happiness. Basically I believe in doing something magical with my time on earth. On top of that, I love love love love people. I love people. And I believe in humanity (it's pretty bad if we humans don't believe in it!). In junior high I filled out a questionnaire that I later found as I was graduating high school, and I said I wanted to be an activist for people with AIDS. I have a very big weak spot for anyone who doesn't have the chances I do, and that's something I plan on dedicating most of my life to. Ideally, I want to incorporate the arts into my efforts in helping others. My sisters call me corny, and I'm ready to accept that! And, as I mentioned earlier...I'm an idealist.

CHRISTINE HAMM (born: 1964): I've been painting since I was three, and writing since kindergarten. I still remember my first story (I was five). It was a horror/fantasy/sci-fi psychological thriller, involving some very round and not so neatly colored creatures called "tabacs." I first attempted to publish at age 7, when I sent a short fiction piece, actually quite derivative of Poe, I'm ashamed to admit, into the kiddie show "Zoom". Like all my work before and since, it was subtly disturbing and darkly humorous. Unfortunately, it was not well received. I was a strange, unwashed, shy, and morbid child, without many friends, and given to planning my funeral in great detail every night before I fell asleep. Perhaps because of this strangeness, and my identification with all peoples and things isolated and maligned, I became a champion of the underdog. All during my childhood and adolescence, I painted oils and watercolor, and wrote odd short stories with unhappy endings. I ended up going to a radical left wing college in the Northwest (Reed), where it was a rite of passage for the freshman boys to grow their hair long, and the freshmen girls to shave their heads. Communism, Atheism, Free Love, was our (un)official college motto, and I lived it to the hilt. I majored in creative writing after dropping my only drawing class. I realized I was not the best artist in the class, so exit was the only viable alternative. This attitude was to haunt me later on. In writing, I was able to convince myself I "might" be the best. I wrote about the real stuff: death, sex, transvestites. My thesis advisor could not restrain himself and eventually had to ask, why don't you write about normal people? Nonetheless, I did grow to become one of the stars of the English Department, which meant I got to have dinner with Katherine Dunn (a Reed graduate) and meet Barbara Ehrenrich (another one). I graduated from said institution a bitter pseudo-intellectual, and immediately started a Master's in Creative Writing at SUNY-Binghamton. During my tenure there, I actually learned how to plot, and also discovered that my particular sympathy for the wounded throbbed around the needy undergrads that I tutored. This experience, also, was to haunt me later.

SANDER HICKS (born: 1971): I incorporated my guerrilla publishing company, Soft Skull Press, in 1996, and went on to publish Michael Stipe, Lee Ranaldo, Eileen Myles, and Dennis Cooper. My plays have also been published by Soft Skull, in two books: *The Breaking Manager* and *Cash Cow & Artanimal.* In June 2000, I accepted the Outstanding Independent Press for Soft Skull at the Firecracker Awards. To date, Soft Skull has published some of the most ground-breaking new political nonfiction, including: *No More Prisons* by William Upski Wimsatt (winner of the Firecracker for Politics in 2000), *Saving Private Power: The Hidden History of "The Good War,"* and the new material for both editions of *Fortunate Son: George W. Bush and the Making of an American President.* In support of

Fortunate Son, I appeared on *60 Minutes, Court TV*, and interviewed with top newspapers and magazines internationally. I'm currently at work on *Kingmaker: The Political Biography of Karl Rove*, for a larger house. Recently Soft Skull produced my play *The Breaking Light* in New York and LA. *The LA Weekly* said this "off-the-wall satire barrels full force toward an absurd little revolutionary war: a capitalist confectionery company vs. a Maoist motivational speaker, an inspired Christian, and Calculatrice, a worker-turned-executive with a visionary candy."

INDIO (born: 1939): January 24, Harlem Hospital, slapped on my ass by this quack after he pulled me out of my mother's womb. Then the dude put me in my mother's arms 'n she allowed me to suck on her breasts. Yeah, I have been a sucker ever since day one. My biological father died when I was two 'n afterwards mother shacked with this black dude, John Calvin Watkins. He was the only father that I knew because they stayed together over thirty-five, up until mother died. I called him "J.C." most of the time 'n he was kool in the game of love with me up until he died. We all lived in Harlem, New York near the Polo Grounds home of the New York Giants baseball 'n football teams back in the day. I was taught my abc's 'n the real deal dealing with society hate games to keep all non whites down. If u wanted to try 'n get by u had 2 act like step n' fechit or be prepared to die. Back in my day when I was around 4 or 5 I asked a lot of questions 'n they would give me good answers except when the questions was too heavy.

They always said: "Good question, Johnny Buck."

"May I have a good answer?"

"Go ask THE GREAT SPIRIT."

I always felt like an ass because I never got an answer 'n that shit made me want to just go suck on mama's lap 'n suck on her tits but I was too fuckin' big 'n old so I would suck on my thumb. Like I says i was a sucker from day one, u dig! Yeah, I learned a lot of the real deal from jump street 'n just loved to be loved by them. Then I went to catholic school 'n believed that "JESUS was comin' to visit every time at mass when I hears bells. It took me a long time to find out that the altar boy was ringin' the bell because I always had my eyes closed—scared that "Jesus" might pick me out 'n take me with him. I was taught that if I went to a non-Catholic church it was a mortal sin 'n should I die, I would go to hell. That shit really hurt J.C. because he was a Baptist 'n wanted to take me to his church sometime but I was brainwashed into that bull-shit thinkin' I would commit a mortal sin 'n would tell him why I couldn't go. Yeah as I started to grow in knowledge, I began to commit a lot of mortal sins in school with the girls. We had sex in the clothes closet, in the boys 'n girls bathrooms, in the basement 'n every place we could get away with it. So, when I graduated from grammar school I had a Ph.D. in sexology. I also won the Best Altar Boy award in 1953. I went to a Catholic high school 'n learned that there was a lot of hate between white Catholics 'n colored Catholics. I had a lot of fights in that school 'n became a member of "The Harlem Lords" to have back-up against those negatives dudes. I graduated in 1957 'n went to city college at night but fell in love 'n got married.

RUSS KICK: Born in 1969, stopped worrying about behaving like an "adult" in 1999. I started writing professionally in 1993. Currently living in Tennessee, of all places. I write articles and books, edit anthologies, run Websites, and do other things involving words in a fact-based (i.e., non-fictional) way. Five books under my belt so far. *Outposts* and *Psychotropedia* are guides to non-mainstream publications, viewpoints, and facts. *Hot Off the Net* is a collection of Internet erotica I edited. *You Are Being Lied To* and *Everything You Know Is Wrong* are anthologies of groundbreaking investigations. http://www.alternewswire.com is my Website for important but neglected or hushed-up news, while Mind Pollen http://www.mindpollen.com/mp.htm is my personal site. I regularly contribute articles to the *Village Voice*, the Disinformation Website http://www.disinfo.com, and *Gauntlet*, the only magazine devoted to free speech issues. My output is on a wide variety of topics, but the underlying theme is an attempt to expose what's being suppressed, get people to question assumptions, make things uncomfortable for those in power, and help information flow freely.

JASON KUCSMA (born: 1974): I have lived in Bowling Green, Ohio for the last 9 years with a one-year stint spent in Laramie, Wyoming. I grew up in the eastside suburbs of Cleveland where I lived a pretty average life as a middle class boy attending Catholic grade school and high school. I got into punk during my senior year in high school, which began my involvement in reading and creating zines as well as being in a punk band and putting on shows for local and traveling bands. I am currently the co-editor/publisher of *Clamor* magazine. I work with my partner Jen Angel to publish *Clamor*, the *Zine Yearbook*, and most recently we have started a non-profit organization called Allied Media Projects. I am also the one of the primary organizers of the annual Underground Publishing Conference—a two-day event geared toward sharing skills for reclaiming media resources. I recently graduated with a master's degree in American Culture Studies where I wrote a thesis about the radicalizing power of punk zines. During my graduate studies, I also taught undergraduate courses in American Culture and Interpersonal Communication.

CHAZ MENA (born: 1966): My parents left Cuba in 1960. They were part of the initial wave of higher to lower middle class Cubans choosing not to participate in Castro's revolution. I was born in NYC six years later. My whole life has been surrounded with storytelling—the one solace afforded to exiles. Cuba was a collection of images, a nostalgic, mythical place rather than a state with an agenda: a faded black & white photograph, a ripe mango, starched white muslin dresses, a worn-out tinny piano playing a *danzones* (Cuban Waltz-like dancing music). I attribute my choosing to become an actor to the necessity of my family to tell stories: I wanted to live them, to protagonist them. So I was raised in Miami, went to school in Pittsburgh, studied theater in Moscow, and moved to NYC in 1996. My wife, whom I adore, was born in Cuba and left with her mom at the age of 4. She is two years younger than me. We have been able to save and buy an apartment (one bedroom) in late 2001.

RICHARD MILLER (born: 1970): I am a non-conformist, atheist vegan with a film degree and the promise of driving an ice cream truck this upcoming summer. I am also a smaller than average, left-handed Gemini who believes in personal freedom and works in a health food store. I live in Queens, NY, where I have resided for the last 8 years. Queens is a good place for a non-traditional thinker; due to its incredible cultural diversity, a casual observer has a very difficult time identifying freaks from cultural newcomers. A place where I can go about my existence in a relatively anonymous fashion while simultaneously despising our government and rejecting Amerikan culture. I was born upstate, just outside of Albany, in 1970. Life was good until 1975 when I was sent to my first year of school. At the time being left-handed was considered to be a sort of correctable birth defect. After a year of staying left-handed in a right-handed world, my family moved about a mile away to a saner district where lefties were merely watched with suspicion rather than outright rejected and beaten. Shortly into my first year of school I learned about the pain of having an ear yanked by an overweight, unhappy, dimwitted teacher who became a sort of model for most of the teachers through my primary school career. I went to film school in Westchester County between 1990 and 1994 where I received a BFA in Motion Picture Directing. After graduating I did manage to break into the film business, and actually had a sort of career in the field for a while, but that wasn't meant to be.

RACHEL MORIELLO (born: 1971): I am an actress, singer, writer, and performance artist living on the upper West Side of Manhattan. I have been living in the city since 1993, when I came here to fulfill my career aspirations. Along the way I have certainly encountered many bumps, particularly around the issue of money, but also around issues of self-worth and changing goals. I am "non-mainstream" in that I have been a vegan for eight years and I am dedicated to producing my own original works of art, whether or not they fall under the category of "commercially successful." I have a group called the Drama Queens. We are female drag queens; we explore gender roles and what it means to be female—or "hyper-female"—in this society, through comedy and music.

CHRISTINA MOSES (born: 1978): I am a black, actually biracial, gay woman. I grew up in Los Angeles, California. I moved here to New York, three and half years ago. Mainly just to be here. It has been my dream to move and live here. Now I realize the fruits of my career are being nurtured here much more powerfully than in any other city, right now. I am an actress, a theatre actress primarily, but I want to give independent films a shot. Defiantly. I am also a photographer and artist. I write and paint...sculpt a bit...My goal is to direct and produce theatre and film documentaries. I love to document and communicate through visuals, music.... I like to take what people don't talk about, what has been talked about and speak to it about in new ways until realities are heard, felt, argued, discussed, and dealt with.

A.D. NAUMAN (born: 1959): I currently live in Chicago where I work as an assistant professor of education. I was born in Lowell, Massachusetts, and grew up in Virginia and Philadelphia. In 1977, I left the east coast to go to college in St. Louis, partly because it was 1000 miles away from my father. In 1987 I moved to Chicago to go to graduate school. I have a Masters in Writing and a Ph.D. in Education from the University of Illinois at Chicago, the architecture of which has been classified as "urban brutalism." I have always been, and always plan to be, a prolific writer. I've published many short stories in literary magazines, won the Illinois Arts Council Literary Award in 1994, and had a story performed by Stories on Stage and broadcast on National Public Radio. *Scorch* is my first published novel, but not the first that I've written. It is, certainly, the best I wrote. My writing is often sociopolitical and satirical. However, I have also written the kind of realistic-personal-experience stories that comprise most of contemporary American fiction, and those are the pieces that tend to get published. I want very much to write and publish fiction that does not go into the slush pile of bourgeois entertainment. I had some difficulty finding an agent for *Scorch*; many agents didn't find it easily enough categorized, and some seemed genuinely confused by it (I'll never forget one agent remarking, in a kind of daze, "It sounds like you're saying consumerism is bad.")

PANAYIOTA PHAROS (born: 1979): I am really bad at doing these things. I was really good in college at writing papers and I always preferred it to other test taking methods, like multiple-choice questions. But I needed to have the question in front of my face throughout my entire writing experience to make sure I was a) answering the question and b) not making any serious digressions (because I tend to totally babble, like I am doing now). With that said, I'm going to create my own question and answer session, and pretend it is an interview with myself (otherwise, I'm bound to go off on serious tangents, like my opinions on Brazilian agriculture and farm life—HELLO). So, here I go:

When did you realize you wanted to be an actor?

Well Nancy (that's a good name for an interviewer, right?), I'm glad you asked that question. Actually, I've always hated that question. I think when people ask it, they expect you to stare dreamily into the sky and say how ever since you were a child you felt God blessed you with this great talent and desire to grace a stage. Not true in my case at all. As a child with my sister and brother, we had a really kick-ass video camera and made these nutty music videos (everything from Jethro Tull's "Benefit" to Poison's "Every Rose has its Thorns" to Run DMC's "Mary Mary") and wacky ass movies with these elaborate plot lines. Of course, this was never considered acting nor did I ever think I would want to do this as a career. Oddly enough, we also used to put on shows for our parents and aunts/uncles during holidays (all of the cousins together). We used to create dance routines and sing along to songs like Twisted Sister's "I Wanna Rock". It was great fun and, of course, being from Greece, our parents had no idea what kind of songs we were singing anyway! But again, not for a career. It was all fun and games. Not until I entered college (Hunter College-CUNY) and took acting classes for elective credits did I actually enjoy it a lot and began to consider it as a career.

GREG RAPAPORT (born: 1966): I'm one of many musicians who feel that they are simply a student of their instrument. I have been playing guitar for over 20 years and in that time have become somewhat of a proficient player but have made no "real" money from playing. I guess what is "non-mainstream" about me is the music that I create. It is essentially a mix of progressive funk and metal fusion. There are no vocals and the music is quite unpredictable so in other words you aren't going to be hearing it on your favorite corporate radio station. My influences come from both the mainstream and "fringe" areas of the music community. Bands such as Led Zeppelin, Yes, and Alice in Chains who are considered commercial, have been big influences in certain aspects of my music. While groups like Tribal Tech, Return to Forever, and Mahavishnu have had a profound effect on me as well. Since my music would never be able to sustain me financially I've started my own small multimedia production company, Splinterhead Productions Inc. I essentially have taken my second passion, art, and have started to make some money out of it. Strategic Marketing Inc. has retained me to head up the multimedia arm of their company. My responsibilities include web development and design, graphic design and layout, video editing, and web animation. I also have created and maintain websites for other musicians as well.

PAMELA RICE (born: 1955): I wasn't exactly a red-diaper baby, but I do come from parents who were fervently against the Viet Nam War, well before anyone else was. This may not seem so remarkable, unless one places my mom and dad in the right wing, up-with-Nixon, lily-white environment of the western suburbs of Chicago, which, unfortunately, is where I grew up. I was raised as a Unitarian in a community where if you didn't have a picture of Jesus on your wall you were a heathen. In our house racism was considered wrong, but the neighborhood where we lived had succeeded utterly in keeping blacks out. And during the sixties I cried at night about the horrors that the United States was inflicting on the people of Viet Nam, while living in a town that was sold on the merits of the domino theory. Left-wing consciousness was passed on to me, but so were a love of writing from my mother and an industrious disposition from my father. Down the road, when I was 35, the ethical and the practical found their apex. This was the year that I became a vegetarian and decided that society could benefit from knowing a lot more about the negative impacts of its meat eating. I set to work! Things got going as soon I wrote the first of five editions of my popular pamphlet, "101 Reasons Why I'm a Vegetarian." (I call it my "mighty convincer.") With the "101 Reasons" I invented myself into a vegetarian street activist. I gave away my pamphlet to NYC pedestrians while wearing a colorful sandwich board and a hat donned with plastic fruit. People frequently wrote back saying that my pamphlet made them rethink their food choices, sometimes drastically. In 1992, I started a vegetarian-issues magazine called *The VivaVine*. Then, some years later, I converted a "basement" vegetarian society into the VivaVegie Society, an official non-profit (www.vivavegie.org). In 1999, I founded the Vegetarian Center of NYC. You might think that a person who believes so strongly in the vegetarian lifestyle might have been born during national fruit-eaters week or something. Quite the contrary: I was born on precisely the same day that Ray Kroc started the McDonald's Corporation, April 15, 1955. Go figure.

MARTA RUSSELL (BORN: 1951): I grew up in the south, in Mississippi, in the fifties and sixties. Born to conservative parents, there was a split in my family when I decided to support civil rights, the integration of black people and protest against the Vietnam War. My father was of the land-owning class and against civil rights; he was pro-military intervention and pro-capitalism. My birth disability, however, gave me great connection to race matters (though I wasn't fully conscious of this until later in life) which would eventually be of use in my work in disability civil rights and my writings on disablement under capitalism.

I started out as an artist/photographer and turned into a radical disability activist. When I moved to Los Angeles after college I got into the visual effects area of film production. I began on Levi's animated ads, on to work on many commercials while at Robert Abel & Associates, and then to other film production companies, including the Walt Disney Co. Later I transitioned into journalism and other writing when my career in the commercial film business ended due to being fired by my then-employer when my impairment progressed and he no longer perceived me as an asset but as a liability.

As an independent producer/journalist, my investigative reporting earned me a Golden Mike Award for Best Documentary from the Southern California Radio and Television News Association in 1995. I was honored as co-producer/correspondent for the KCET Life & Times documentary entitled, "Disabled & the Cost of Saying 'I Do'" on marriage disincentives in Social Security policy.

My commentaries have been published in the *San Jose Mercury News, the Los Angeles Times, the San Diego Union Tribune, the Austin American-Statesman* and other newspapers around the nation. My academic work focuses on the socio/economic aspects of disablement and has been published in the *Berkeley Journal of Employment and Labor Law, Review of Radical Political Ecomony, Journal of Disability Policy Studies, Monthly Review Magazine,* and *Disability and Society.* Disability policy and commentaries have appeared in *New Mobility Magazine, Ragged Edge, Mouth, the voice of disability rights,* and *Z Magazine,* among others.

My first book, *Beyond Ramps, Disability at the End of the Social Contract* (Common Courage Press, 1998), a condemnation of disablement under capitalism, received an Honorable Mention from the Outstanding Books Awards presented by the Gustavus Myers Program for the Study of Bigotry and Human Rights in North America at Boston University.

I have a daughter who is a student at UCLA and I live in Los Angeles, California.

SUSANA SANTIZO (born: 1980): I was born in Guatemala. My parents Sylvana and Jorge did their best to support their three children in a Third World country without prostituting themselves (drug trafficking, stealing, joining the Mafia or the corrupt and often fatal military). They struggled to put food on the table and then headed out to New York. The trip took three months by bus, car, train, and foot. I spent my first birthday in L.A. Coming here "illegally" was the best decision my parents had ever made. Approving a visa took too many years. I would've been a child selling homemade products in the street with the potential to become a great teacher of life and no opportunity to use it. Is there anything sadder? Despite the circumstances I grew up very fortunate. My parents were always working (Mami cleaned houses; Papi was a cook in a nursing home and he occasionally worked in factories) but our needs were always met and we had three meals a day. I made a promise long ago. I would become a teacher, not just someone with a degree. Someone who found the truth in so many lies and wants to share it with everybody. My writing inspires me every day, to see that no one could ever take any credit for showing me my outstanding love for truthful words. I am very proud of myself! I know I will accomplish what I always said I would do. Show the world that life is only worth living when you discover the worth of living, I will do it going against the grain and I will create a stronger new one.

MANNY SIVERIO (born: 1960): I am a Hispanic-American living in Astoria. I am a Stunt Coordinator, Stunt Man, Writer, Webmaster, Actor, 2nd Unit Director, Martial Artist, Mambo Instructor and Mambo Performer who is a member of SAG, DGA, AFTRA and the WGA. I am also a member of Stunt Specialist (an East Coast Stunt Organization) and HOLA (Hispanic Organization of Latin Artists). I like to see myself as an example of the modern-Latino Renaissance man. A jack of all trades. Actually everything seems to stem off of my martial arts foundation (writer, stunting, directing, even dancing).

SPARROW (born: 1953): I suppose you would call me a writer. That is, words in configurations appear in magazines, newspapers, and books with my name on them. Actually, I do not consider myself a writer; in part because I have carpal tunnel syndrome, plus golf elbow *and* tennis elbow (as the result of too much typing.) Thus, I write very little—that is, I do not operate pen or keyboard. What I am doing at this moment is speaking into a voice-activated computer. I am, to be exact, a person who lies in bed, thinks for a while, then walks into the living room and speaks into his computer.

I keep the Jewish Sabbath (although I do turn lights off and on). From Friday night to Saturday night I do not spend money, ride in a car, use the computer, turn on the radio. I read, talk, think in bed.

My politics are democratic socialist, though most people believe I'm an anarchist, because I dress extremely poorly. I oppose capitalism, which seems to me justified slavery. I consider myself a revolutionary, but am dubious about violence as a useful scheme.

TIM WISE (born: 1968): I am a Southern-based white antiracism activist and essayist, who organizes, harangues, lectures, and generally causes trouble on college campuses, and in communities all across the United States. Since the age of fourteen I have been speaking out against institutional and individual white supremacy and racism in education, the job market, politics, U.S. foreign policy and the justice system. I was a principal activist in the anti-David Duke campaigns in Louisiana in the early 1990s and my syndicated columns are carried by ZNet and Alternet. I have done antiracism trainings for law enforcement, school boards, and even the Ford Motor Company: most of which smiled, paid me, and then ignored the things I said, but which occasionally have made real changes in their operations, and for that I'm grateful.

MICKEY Z. (born: 1960): I reside with my wife, Michele, in Astoria where I've lived for my entire life. I am the author of *Saving Private Power: The Hidden History of "The Good War"* (Soft Skull Press) and *Forgotten New York: Small Slices of a Big Apple* (Seaburn Books). My writing has also appeared in two books from Disinformation: *You Are Being Lied To* and *Everything You Know is Wrong*. During my twenty-plus years of staining paper with ink, I was the editor-in-chief of *Curio* magazine and a regular columnist for *Street News*; I've been quoted in the *New York Times*, I've optioned three film screenplays, I've edited five of my own zines (*The Flaming Crescent, Endgame, Sil Lum Tao, Cool Observer*, and *Mickey Z. Says*) and co-edited another (*Out of Bounds*), I've authored two poetry chapbooks and three DIY political pamphlets, I was known as the "underground poet" because I hung my words in the subway, I've written for a wide range of publications from anarchist magazines to Conde Nast glossies (subjects have included police brutality, vegetarianism, kung fu, chess, film, garlic, Fabio, and the Society to Eradicate Television), I was the managing editor of a third-rate girlie magazine, I've written several novels—none of which have been published yet. I was awarded a fellowship in non-fiction literature from the New York Foundation for the Arts in 1997 and got a grant from the Puffin Foundation in 2002. I just started as Senior Editor of *Wide Angle*—so stay tuned. While I'm sure I've left a few things out, I think you get the idea: in the field I've chosen, there is no formula. As a result, to quote Groucho, I've worked my way up from nothing to a state of extreme poverty. Let me put it this way: I don't wear black; I don't smoke, drink, or do drugs—nor do I sleep till noon (or even stay up past ten at night). My organically-fueled body is free of tattoos and piercings, I does not own a weapon or belong to a sect, and I am happily and faithfully married. However, while my "vices" aren't drugs or guns or mysticism or sexual deviance (well, maybe a little sexual deviance), my lifestyle is far more controversial to the establishment. I don't eat their food or worship their god or accept their government. I also don't visit their doctors or take their medicines or use their deodorants, colognes, toothpastes, etc.; I don't have their accepted academic credentials; and I don't drive their cars, engage in conspicuous consumption, or create unnecessary waste. In addition, I try not to purchase items I know to be made by slave or sweatshop labor. In other words, if everyone were like me, the corporate commodity culture would vanish overnight. This simple reality makes me far more menacing and radical than I first appear. Perhaps my inability to make a living as a writer in a world inundated with words is the ultimate proof of this thesis.

You keep hearing that society's greatest tasks are educating people and getting them jobs. That's great. Two things people hate to do: go to school and go to work.
—GEORGE CARLIN

LIKE A VIRGIN

(FIRST JOBS AND OTHER AWAKENINGS)

SANDER HICKS: When I was 13 I started to work the summers in the snack bar of the suburban pool club behind my house. It was cool, because I had access to all of this candy and ice cream. I also liked handling cash and the stress of taking orders, making change, and running a deep fat fryer and grill, sometimes all at once. But I also learned some valuable lessons about the suppression of wages by capitalists. The snack bar was run by a suburban father who paid us $2 an hour. I guess he figured we wanted to work at the pool, and we did...but it's illegal to pay kids below minimum wage if they aren't related to you, isn't it? Even today, working construction out here in Long Island, I got fired and almost shot by the boss last weekend because he fought with me about the hours I'd worked. He didn't want to pay us for the time it took us to travel to the jobs. Really he was mad we couldn't cut through this steel column that day.

CHAZ MENA: My wife Ileana and I embarked on a venture to make and sell jewelry: necklaces, anklets, and lockets. We had contracted friends to help us manufacture the jewelry. It turned out to be a pyramid scam where the bottom fell out. She and I were suddenly in hock for $17,000. It was a desperate plan to raise money for our move to New York City.

SUSANA SANTIZO: I was a peer educator in my neighborhood community center. Ten of us would sit and discuss the problems that affected our community and how we could slow down the process. After many meetings and thorough research we put on a conference in schools. I definitely loved this job, I always have an opinion and I loved writing the lectures and skits for the conferences. It was also the lowest paying job (aren't they always?).

MANNY SIVERIO: When I was 18, I taught in a small karate school in Hatillo, Puerto Rico and when I got back to New York—I was born in Brooklyn—I started the Modern Combat in Action (MCIA) School of Fighting. I'm indebted to my mother for scraping up the money to pay for my lessons. She didn't know how far it would go.

CHRISTINE HAMM: After I graduated from SUNY-Binghamton, I moved to NYC, hoping to make it big as a writer while I worked in publishing. Cue laugh track. My first awful misconception was that publishing had something to do with literature, rather than sales. The second was that I could somehow get published myself. After a year as a lowly editorial assistant, a year of subsisting on baloney sandwiches, I decided to become a secretary and I got a ten thousand dollar raise. I also got free tuition at NYU, and I was accepted to the Ph.D. program in Literature there. In the context of Spanish Harlem, where I was living, and the psychiatric hospitalization of someone very close to me the atmosphere of the ivory tower soon seemed self-indulgent and irrelevant. After much thought, I transferred to NYU's graduate school of social work. I became an advocate for the homeless and mentally ill, and worked in a shelter for homeless women. However, at the same time, it was difficult for me to find the time and energy to continue working on my art. Spending all day trying to convince screaming schizophrenics to take their medication was emotionally and mentally exhausting. All I could do after work was prop open my eyelids and click on the WB. This went on for seven years. I finally took some courses at the School of Visual of Arts. In the war between Christine the activist and Christine the artist, the artist won. Or so I thought. I quit social work to study and work in the field of graphic design. But I was unable to find anything remotely related to that area, and I was forced to be a secretary.

RICHARD MILLER: I was 16 years old when I took a job doing an early cleaning shift at my local McDonald's. My coworker Bob did menial labor in between smuggling runs from Hawaii to the mainland. My stay at this job was short. Cleaning the prep and kitchen stations lasted about 6 weeks for me, culminating in an invite to try Bob's Hawaiian gig. I declined the offer and found other work. It is sometime around this point in my life that I picked up an essential skill to the survival of almost any American. I took a job washing dishes at an Italian restaurant. Dishwashing is perhaps the shittiest job available today, it includes garbage, mopping, and hauling old food; it really puts into perspective the unfairness of life. This is a skill most of the wealthy will never possess, it is the property of the working class. That's what makes it essential to your average American misfit; it belongs to us. I took this skill onto several other establishments culminating in a stint in the kitchen at a local country club. Country clubs are amazing places to work, they even allow minorities in the kitchens these days; at least they did at Norman's Hill where I worked. Eventually, after about a year, I was doing some prep work and fewer dishes. All the while I earned minimum wage, $3.35 an hour at the time. The thing about working in kitchens is that you get to see the food business up close, and it's dirty and nasty, not to mention full of alcoholic drug abusers. Ah, but what a good place to pilfer. Anyone who works in a kitchen and has to buy food is doing something wrong.

INDIO: I worked at my father's glass store, then Port Authority as a baggage man unloadin' the bags from the bus, then worked at Chase Manhattan Bank, Bank of Boston International, J.H. Schroder Banking Corporation, Atlantic Bank of New York 'n Chemical Bank.

A.D. NAUMAN: Waitress, phone solicitor (for about 3 weeks), secretary (at several places, for about 3 weeks each), tour boat commentator, teacher, newspaper stringer, copy editor, administrative assistant, freelance medical editor, freelance writer. My editorial skills got me a few oddball jobs, like editing a professor's book about impoverished women in a writing class in the San Francisco Tenderloin area. Once I edited a textbook about death. Another time, my mom made a contact for me in her town, Lafayette, Indiana—a gynecologist there wanted help with an article he was trying to publish. So I went to have a consultation with him, at a place called the Women's Health Center, which—no lie—is constructed as two big domes with nipple-like points on top. No one is sure if the design was intentional or subconscious. Once, out of pity, my dad hired me to run errands for him. I did that for about a month, and couldn't have paid my rent otherwise. That year my total income was $4000. I worked on several short stories and a novel, but the writing never went well. Money worries and job-hunting absorbed so much mental energy. The horrible jobs I did have were so demoralizing, such a blow to my confidence, I wasn't able to be very creative. That was the year I was living in Washington, D.C., for no real reason. I was right out of college, with my degree in English literature, qualified for nothing. One of the major employers in Washington D.C. are the associations; I did a 3-week stint as a secretary for the Association of Municipal Finance Officers (good God, I can hardly stay awake through the phrase). My boss, a very pushy, short, loud woman, complained that I didn't look cheerful enough.

SETH ASHER: I was an accountant from early 1986 to late 1987 at Spicer & Oppenheimer. At the time I was eager to "get ahead." However, even back then, I did realize that the work was absurdly meaningless and depressing. It was a difficult realization that required all of my denial capacities to keep going at it for the sake of advancement.

SPARROW: The first job I ever had was at an Associated Supermarket on Nagle Avenue, in my neighborhood (Inwood: the most uptown section of Manhattan). I was 15 years old. My job was to bag groceries, and stock the shelves. I saw another worker eating a fruit pie, and I asked: "Are we allowed to eat the food?" He said yes, so I took a Tastycake. The boss noticed, and later interrogated me. "Someone told me I could have a snack," I explained. "Who told you?" he asked. I paused. Then I said: "Jose" (to my endless shame). The boss fired both of us. This was July 4, 1969. I walked home as fireworks shot off around me. That was my first day of work. Three weeks later I was working at Pathmark, another—much larger—supermarket on 207th Street. I was in "maintenance." This meant that when a bottle broke, they called me to the afflicted aisle, and I rushed with my mop and bucket. First I collected the glass, then mopped, then searched for extra shards. I remember a particular broken bottle of white vinegar clearly. The job was cautious, absurd, and generous; I was protecting children, old men, and women from lacerating injury. Sometimes a box of detergent fell, and smashed. That was much easier work.

CHRISTINA MOSES: My first job? I was 16. I had to pay for my 1974 Volvo, the insurance and a new set of tires. My mother got me a job at Universal Studios Hollywood at the photo booth. We were the ones responsible for all those goofy photos of the theme park characters and all the tourists; you know characters like, Frankenstein and the Mummy. I sold them! I had to wear a uniform. A bright blue turquoise collar shirt and shorts of my choice provided they were preppy and clean. It was great. I had to learn to drive my standard 1974 Volvo up a *huge* hill everyday for the summer. I stalled a lot, rolled backwards a lot, but I learned how to drive as I learned how to work. I had a lot of fun there. I mean it was cheesy beyond belief, but I paid for my car and took care of it all by myself.

GREG RAPAPORT: I started working when I was 13 moving furniture over the summer. During junior high and part of high school I vacuumed floors at a lingerie store. The rest of high school I worked at a local department store, cleaning and stocking shelves. The department store was probably my biggest "sell-out" job because I had to kiss the customers' asses as well as the boss's. The clientele were snobs and frequently asked me if I could come over to their house and clean their bathrooms and vacuum their floors. Apparently this was their feeble attempt at humor. Not funny. I remember taking quite a bit of verbal abuse from one of the boss's sons pretty frequently. He was a rich spoiled brat. At that point he was in his early 30's, married with a kid. He enjoyed threatening my job and degrading me. (Hmmm, that may be the root of my authority problem.)

MICKEY Z.: My first after-school job was delivering the long-defunct *Long Island Press* but I really entered the working world when I started as a temporary summer worker at the age of seventeen at Gimbel's department store (my Dad knew someone there—lucky me). Wow, the *Long Island Press* and Gimbel's: how 1970s of me. Anyway, I eased my way into the good graces of the bosses until I got into the union. Ultimately, I maneuvered myself into a Sunday-only work schedule. This arrangement enabled me to only work seven hours a week at a union-enforced double-time wage and thereby garnered me enough cool cash in seven lousy hours to easily finance my youthful—and very inexpensive—existence. Still, being the anti-authority type of fellow I am, I wasn't satisfied and I soon figured out a way to sign myself in and out at lunch time and spend most of my time across the street in Macy's, watching football in their crowded television department after a terribly un-nourishing lunch at the Blimpie's on 32nd Street (I didn't even know what a vegan was yet). At Gimbel's, I got to spend a lot of time with some older guys who did this kind of menial work for a living and I gained some valuable insight into the typical worker-employee relationships I could look forward to in my future enslavements.

GARY BADDELEY: When I left school I didn't want to go to university (I later reversed that decision) and applied for a job at Harrods, the posh department store in London. I thought I'd be a shoe-in for an easy sales job. I guess they had me figured out though, and offered me a temporary job as a seasonal furniture porter. It was a pretty easy job actually. In three months I was able to read the whole of *War and Peace* and several other books. What I remember most about the job (other than it's being boring) was that after the IRA bombed Harrods there were numerous bomb scares. We were expected to look in all the furniture for bombs. Yeah, right!

MARTA RUSSELL: Before cracking into the film business I picked up any employment I could. I worked as a bartender for a while. One night I "auditioned" for bartender job at the Palamino Club in North Hollywood, a legendary Hollywood club now defunct. After working for free the entire night to show how I could perform (I wondered how much free labor the Palamino's manager got by making people "try out" for the competitive job as bartender there) I was followed by a customer out the door. As I started my car, he started his. He chased me down the streets of the San Fernando Valley: Lankershim Blvd., Burbank Blvd,, Laurel Canyon, Victory Blvd. until I could finally evade him by turning enough corners to lose him in traffic. The Palamino Club manager didn't warn me that the female bartenders there were subject to harassment off the premises.

RUSS KICK: In 1992-93, I ran mail-order catalog for alternative books, which flopped. It started as a computer BBS (bulletin board system—those were the pre-Web days), and then became a catalog on paper. I had to sell my entire Beatles collection, including John and Yoko's infamous *Two Virgins* album, just to keep it (and myself) afloat. That only prolonged the inevitable.

PAMELA RICE: Just barely out of college, a placement counselor (head-huntress) got me a job as a secretary in the research and development department at a major mattress manufacturer. I kid you not. I think it was Sealy, but I can't be sure. (This goes back to the late 1970s.) I worked at the famed Merchandise Mart in Chicago, which was probably the best part of this sad episode. Before me, the job had been held by a guy who, through creativity and ingenuity, fashioned the position into something quite grander than what I was getting into. The job had been sold to me on the premise that I too could possibly fashion something grand out of the job. On day one, I realized that this was not in the cards. While the other guy had been "fashioning," he had been neglecting mountains of drudgery for the person coming after him: me. Then, I got all kinds of signals from one of the R & D engineers I was secretary for; one might call it sexual harassment. I tattled on him, which probably messed his life up plenty. The situation had to be "handled," as I recall. Ultimately, I got out of there, not even a week after I started, and back to the job-interviewing merry-go-round. Ugh.

JEN ANGEL: Well, I've been working since I was 14 when I got a job at the library next to the high school, so I've had a lot of jobs. Somehow, I've managed to never have a food service job. I've worked at a library, a recycling center, a paint manufacturer, a video store, a manufacturer of hospital sterilizers, a printing press, a record distribution, a construction engineering firm, a record store, and I've done short temp-work stints at dozens of other crappy places. Almost every job I have had would fall into the secretary/file clerk/office peon type role, because most of the "employable" skills I have involve being able to use computers and office equipment well.

TIM WISE: Before graduating I worked in the summers as a canvasser for Greenpeace, which was political only in theory. Basically, it was a bullshit fundraising position, with almost no political substance at all: going door to door and pissing people off at dinnertime, asking them to give me $25 for a magazine, but acting as if their contribution was the difference between whale survival versus whale genocide. Absolute bullshit. Never addressed local environmental issues; always talking about goddamned tuna fishermen catching dolphins in their nets, or Icelandic whalers: never anything that was closely linked to local struggles, just abstract stuff that most people just laugh at. We would have demonstrations at the goddamned Burger King, not to protest the deforestation that these fast food companies engage in so as to graze cattle (which at least would have been a direct linkage), but instead to protest the fucking fish sandwich because it was Icelandic fish, and some Icelandic fishermen still kill whales. Talk about abstract. No wonder Greenpeace is such a moribund group nowadays, and their canvassing offices all but a memory: this is the kind of bullshit that they considered vital activism. Anyway, it paid like shit. One-third of what you raised, with a quota to meet in order to even get that. My heart wasn't in it, but my co-workers were nice and fun so I stuck with it. I usually made no money in a given week, or just very little. But since it was summer, and I was still in school, I was living at home and didn't need too much. The only decent part of the whole thing was the people, and the parties we'd have every week, which were basically an excuse to get high.

SPARROW: I flunked out of Cornell University in 1973. Soon after, I worked in construction; my friend Brad found me the job. "You dig a good ditch," my supervisor told me. (This boss had the talent to fall asleep at lunchtime, and wake up exactly when lunch was over.) I cleaned up the cell-like rooms we were constructing, on a hilltop near Ithaca. When the other workers left a room, I would collect the little colored wires and rug lint that remained. My girlfriend and I hitchhiked down to St. Petersburg, Florida, where we lived in a boarding house. (This was 1974.) I worked in a sheet metal factory producing the display boxes in front of churches that reveal the next sermon. I came home with metal splinters in my fingers. The boss was a short man who walked around talking to himself. My one friend was an older woman who was always reading lurid books about Indian massacres. "Let's go streaking around the factory today," she once said. This was the first I heard of streaking—the practice of running around naked, as a joke. Joan and I moved to Gainesville, Florida. I answered an ad for a job at a "truss factory"; I assumed this meant manufacturing girdles, but actually they built "house trusses." These are big wooden V-shaped supports for roofs. I worked with a number of people from a local prison. With one of them (I forget his name) I lunched every day. One day he tried to kiss me. This frightened me. One thing I hated about that job was having to "look busy." We worked outdoors, behind a big platform on which the trusses lay. Even when there were no trusses, we were supposed to walk around hammering in stray nails on the platform, and appearing competent. I was not good at this "ad-libbing." Also at that job, the locals once asked me if I ate pussy. I admitted that I did, and every lunchtime after that they inquired if I had brought "pussy sandwich."

Now I got a job, but it don't pay.
—THE CLASH

PASSING INSPECTION

(RESUMES AND INTERVIEWS)

WHAT'S THE BIGGEST LIE ON YOUR RESUME?

GARY BADDELEY: I don't have a resume! With the exception of my first job out of law school, I never needed one.

RACHEL MORIELLO: On my acting resume it says I weigh 119 lbs. That is a lie.

RUSS KICK: That I'm a team player.

PAMELA RICE: No lies. I don't believe in it. I suppose it's hurt me in my career.

CHRISTINE HAMM: I leave out my short-term jobs (stuff under a month).

MANNY SIVERIO: In my business I can't have lies. They are easy to check up. If someone finds a lie on your resume, they'll never trust anything you say from that point on. I've had people tell me that they've worked on projects that I coordinated. When I bust them, they know they'll never work for me again.

JEN ANGEL: I actually don't lie on my resume. How lame is that? I guess I omit certain details: like jobs I don't want them to know about, or people I don't want them to call.

SANDER HICKS: I just re-read it. I hate to break it to you, but everything on it is true.

GREG RAPAPORT: Didn't have a resume until a few years ago. Haven't lied on it yet.

SUSANA SANTIZO: I always write as one of my skills, "able to give and take orders." I suck at both.

MICKEY Z.: You'd never know how many times I've been fired. Plus, there's absolutely no mention of pornography and I have been known to claim to have a college degree (to no avail, I might add).

TIM WISE: Nowadays there are none. I'm lucky enough to have a good reputation for what I do, so I stopped lying about things like that years ago. There used to be some minor ones, but I've been able to purge those. Oh, well, except the part about being 6'3" and a championship skier: but that's not a lie, so much as a complete and splendid fabrication, or perhaps creative writing.

MARTA RUSSELL: I don't bother with a resume anymore. Now I just send out a list of all the work that has been published. No lies, just the facts ma'am.

SANDER HICKS: Okay, looking over this resume, I realize it DOES shave some corners. It claims I was "CEO" of Soft Skull Press for five whole years. I was always the founder and a top director, but the title of CEO was tossed around between me, Susan Mitchell and Stuart Bagwell, two crazy founding partners, whom I'd outlasted and out-crazied for five years. What do they say about the victors writing history?

DO YOU HAVE ANY GOOD INTERVIEW STORIES?

PAMELA RICE: It's painful to think back at all the interviews I've been on. It's ungodly, really. At one point after a particularly long unemployment and what seemed like zillions of interviews, I got into sales. As a sales rep I did a lot of cold calling and setting up interviews. It seemed so natural by this time: making arrangements to meet with people, going up to their offices, shooting the breeze, negotiating, getting disappointed, and sometimes making deals. Kind of like when I was unemployed!

MANNY SIVERIO: On one film, when this big time director interviewed me, he insisted on telling me how Puerto Ricans dress. "Lots of bright colors," he said. Another time, I was up for a role but the director—another big name—told me I "didn't look Hispanic enough."

PANAYIOTA PHAROS: There's nothing really funny or interesting about any job interviews/auditions that I've been on. You'd think the job interview for the dating service would be a wild one, but it was actually quite normal. It wasn't until after I got the job that I really realized what kind of clientele I was dealing with.

SANDER HICKS: I have conducted several job interviews, and I think one of the best questions you can ask someone is "How do your friends describe you?" because it indicates a lot about self-image. I was looking for a web-designer at one point, and this candidate's answer was "a rock star." I actually thought that was really cool, but the guy never called me back. I guess he got other offers.

GREG RAPAPORT: I've never gone on an interview.

SUSANA SANTIZO: I once answered an ad in the paper for "social butterflies" thinking it had something to do with clubs. I was desperate. I went to the interview and he had 4 of us in the room, he said he would ask us a question and he would eliminate one person after we answered all the questions that had to do with our drive for success. I was the last one there. I was so excited to think he picked me. The next day at my new job I found out I would be soliciting in the streets of N.Y. I told him to find another fucking butterfly.

RUSS KICK: The worst question you can possibly get is, "What would you say your greatest weakness is?" I can't even remember how I've answered this; probably something like, "I work too hard," or, "I'm a perfectionist." These are basically the only ways you can answer that question and still have a prayer of getting the job. A couple of years ago on a lark, my friend Darrell and I came up with a list of snappy answers to that stupid interview question. Here are some of my favorite replies to "What is your greatest weakness?"

I am prone to random acts of violence.

I like to sleep on the job.

I'm a cokehead and go on weekend binges. Sometimes I don't make it in until Tuesday.

I don't like people.

I don't file things ... I've been known to just trash paperwork.

I'll sell the companies secrets to the highest bidder.

I piss in the office coffee pot.

I can't read good.

I use the company car to pick up hookers.

I comment on female employees' breast size.

I sometimes like to masturbate in my office.

My college degree is from a diploma mill.

I think it's a weakness that I'm forced to consider working here.

I don't have any weaknesses. I'm fucking perfect!

JEN ANGEL: I just hate when you apply for you a job and you interview and it sounds great, but at the end they come back and tell you that the pay is half what you were making at your previous job and it's only 25 hours a week anyway. Why can't they just be upfront with how much they will pay? I've been to a lot of interviews around here where I know I want to make $10.00 per hour, but I can't call and say, "How much do you pay?" before going on the interview. I have to go to the interview it, have them like me, and have them call and offer me 7 or 8 dollars an hour. Its just frustrating because I'm 27, I have a college degree, etc. I've developed a lot of skills (mostly through my extra curricular activities like doing zines) that could be an asset. If I made more money or were able to work less hours per week and still support myself, it would be easier to work on my other projects more. I read a survey last year that the average college graduate in Ohio makes $18 per hour. Fuck, not where I come from. I have a degree and tons of experience, and it's a struggle to get a job that makes more than $10.

TIM WISE: Well, before I took the wine-stocking gig, I interviewed for a lot of other ones, and never got an offer. I would be asked things like: "So, tell me why you think it would be fun to sell bottled water," or "So, what attracted you to the telemarketing profession," or, "So, how long have you wanted a career in multi-level marketing." And I would either start laughing or I would say something sarcastic like, "Well, I've dreamt of selling soap with Amway since I was at least seven: it's a lifelong dream." Not too good for landing a job, you know?

SPARROW: I have had very few job interviews. The worst I can remember is a woman who looked at my resume and said: "I just have one question: how do you make a living?"

SUSANA SANTIZO: I had a women tell me that she didn't believe in equal opportunity employment and then asked me if I thought I was good enough for the position. I told her I was too good.

Artist Schmartist, ya can't be supported all ya life.
—LEO KEROUAC TO HIS SON JACK

HIDDEN TALENTS

(UNUSUAL QUALIFICATIONS)

PAMELA RICE: If you have a cause that appears to be a loser, put me on the job. Quixotic is my middle name.

RACHEL F.: I love doing calligraphy. That's another option. I could create wedding invitations; I would advertise in elegant stationery stores. There's not enough time to do all of the things that would be appealing.

SPARROW: I can offer potential employers an immaterial sense of humor, good art criticism, an ability to organize failed performance events, patience, mortality.

SANDER HICKS: I'm always thinking about how to improve things, how to put procedures into place that are self-improving, empowering to those involved, and reproductive. I was thinking today, we have to have a revolutionary movement that is reproductive. If the revolution could be developed into something that reproduces itself, then it would be undefeatable.

MARTA RUSSELL: Let's see. I bring my own chair to work.

PAMELA RICE: I know how to turn a complex factual point into a succinct paragraph. I got a hundred of 'em.

RICHARD MILLER: I'm the perfect person for a corporation to hire to find out what's gonna fail. I can pick a loser right every time—from my heart. If you wanna find out who *not* to market something to, ask me.

MICKEY Z.: I can play note-for-note air guitar to all of Edward Van Halen's solos (pre-Sammy).

SPARROW: I know how to put on a Band-Aid, and how to play intuitive harmonica.

PAMELA RICE: I'm able to detect a meat eater just by the way he or she smells.

TIM WISE: I have no such qualifications, and have not the temperament to work for anyone. It is for that reason that I (fortunately for me and for anyone for whom I might work) am self-employed.

SANDER HICKS: I like both aggressive growth, and revolution. Combine two tastes into one and end up with the super worker's result.

PANAYIOTA PHAROS: I wouldn't really call any of my qualifications "unusual" or maybe that's the unusual part: that I think I could say with a good level of confidence that I am quite normal. I can't prepare split pea soup and jump on one foot at the same time or make screeching noises that would remind people of rare African sea birds (and I'm assuming here that because I'm an actress, a potential employer would be a casting director). The only thing I can offer is myself: my desire to learn, my willingness to dig deep, and the satisfaction of bringing a character to life. Yup, I'm just a normal chick living in Queens trying to get people to notice! Maybe I should take up some sort of hobby to spice myself up— like some sort of sushi-circus class or something.

GREG RAPAPORT: I'm a very hard worker. I'm also very creative. Everybody is better off if I'm left alone to do my work. I hate corporate politics and would not get involved in them. I don't kiss ass, sorry.

PAMELA RICE: I know how to placate policemen. This comes from many years of being asked to fold up and move my outreach educational table off of a public sidewalk.

RACHEL MORIELLO: I can be extremely charming when I want to be (that was my problem with bartending: I was expected to be that all the time and I wasn't! I would tell the customers MY problems.)

INDIO: Have a Ph. D. in Streetology, Sexology 'n Homelessnessology.

PAMELA RICE: I know the technical difference between a vegetarian and a vegan. I also have many years experience answering the question: "How will I get enough protein if I become a vegetarian?"

MANNY SIVERIO: My experience as a club bouncer has given me an eye to create a more real and viciously artistic violent fight scene. I know when it's time to be in charge and when to step back. I know what my job is, when to do it, and when to step back and not be in the way. I let producers know that I'm there to fulfill what the director wants when he knows what he wants, but I'm also there to help the director when doesn't know what he wants because he doesn't have the experience. So depending on the director, I'm there to be another tool at his disposal or to be a silent partner (an not make him feel incompetent). Finally, I tell a producer to look at my resume and that should them help understand that I've been around the block a couple of times.

PAMELA RICE: I am able to sound enthusiastic when someone, usually a person I hardly know, tells me the details of their constipation and how it went away after he or she adopted a vegetarian diet.

RACHEL F.: You can trust me with your keys.

PAMELA RICE: I have ferreted out dozens of ways that the meat industry is subsidized by the government. Since most of these giveaways are hidden or nearly invisible, I count this as one of my more valuable abilities.

GARY BADDELEY: Given that any likely employer of mine is likely to be in the entertainment industry, I'm probably one of the few candidates who could work for virtually any entertainment company: I have direct experience, both as an operating executive and on the business and legal affairs side, in recorded music, music publishing, talent management, television production and distribution, book publishing, internet publishing, online commerce, and I hope to produce a movie in the near future. The only area that I'm really ignorant about is video games. I'd like to get into that too.

PAMELA RICE: An extra bonus: I can explain to large groups the intricacies of how to recycle.

INDIO: I will always come to work ready for a rough day! Why? Every morning, I ask my American pit bull dog, Rex, "What kind of a day will I have?" 'n he sezs: RUFF!

PAMELA RICE: I know just how to wear a head stocking donned with plastic fruit; there's an art to this, you know.

Children are smarter than any of us. Know how I know that? I don't know one child with a full time job and children.
—BILL HICKS

GIGS

BEST, WORST, AND EVERYTHING IN-BETWEEN

BEST

SUSANA SANTIZO: I love working with children. It comes second to my writing. I've been working with kids for years at Steppingstone Day School and nothing makes me feel as satisfied as knowing I made a difference in a child's life. I sincerely mean that. I leave work every day happy, with the hope of a better tomorrow. It keeps me in check. I understand myself better and realize there is a bigger picture.

JASON KUCSMA: I do production work, some design and some customer service. It's a great job, because there are only two employees and the owner. I have enough responsibility there that I feel important, but not so much that I feel obligated to put in extra hours when I don't have time to necessarily do so. The hours are somewhat flexible, which is really important during the times when *Clamor* demands more time and attention from us (i.e. during the peak production periods of each issue).

TIM WISE: After college I walked into the dream job: working for the main anti-David Duke organization when he was running for US Senate and for Governor of Louisiana. I was lucky: I had gone to school in New Orleans and the group was founded by a history professor of mine, as well as an activist colleague on campus. I started off organizing college students against Duke, and eventually became Assistant Director. It was amazing: very high-profile, especially for a 22 year old. High pressure; death threats from Nazis every day. Learned a lot, and that really has made the difference in my career.

GEORGIA GIANNIKOURIS: I had a job that I absolutely loved. I was so happy with it! I was teaching at an after-school program in a city school. This program, called LEAP (Learning through an Extended Arts Program), was amazing. We were all hired to teach anything we wanted to children between kindergarten and fifth grade. I taught theater, creative writing, jewelry making, and peer leadership. That was one of the most fulfilling of all jobs! I felt so at peace with myself. I was teaching things that I was in love with, and the students were so eager to learn! I was making very little money, and I worked very few hours, but I wouldn't trade it for the world. It was a sacrifice, but it was worth it. The only problem was that you end up in a Catch-22. I was doing something I loved, but I never had enough money to do other things I equally loved. By that time we had moved to New Jersey, and I was paying ten bucks a day for buses and trains to get there. I'm not one to complain, and I always go out of my way to make the best of a situation, so it barely bothered me, but it wasn't so easy. There are quick money jobs, and there are soul-satisfying careers. Right now I'm in between.

SPARROW: I do enjoy my present job—as a substitute teacher at a Catskills high school. (Although I am also a journalist, I don't see this as a "job"—more as a manic hobby. Perhaps because I love journalism, and spend hours a day addictively reading old copies of the *New York Press*.) I have a special "ministry" with the punks and goth kids, to reassure them that anti-intellectualism is a valid, even spiritual, life-option. Plus I read my latest poetry aloud to them.

GARY BADDELEY: My best job is my current one: President of The Disinformation Company. There's nothing like controlling your own destiny.

WORST

PANAYIOTA PHAROS: I think I've worked in every aspect of customer service that's available. I worked retail at Lord & Taylor—the worst job of my life—I can't ever walk into a department store without cringing.

GREG RAPAPORT: My worst job was vacuuming at the lingerie store—the boss was a Hitleresque asshole. The best job is the job I have now, because I'm the asshole.

MARTA RUSSELL: All jobs are wage slavery but some worse than others. My worst job and my biggest sell-out job were the same job in my case. I was hired as the production manager for a commercial film production house in Los Angeles. This meant that I oversaw the production of music videos as well as corporate commercials for about six directors. I was the owner's point woman to keep things under budget and on time. It was a sell-out job because I detest commercials in the first place. Some may think music videos are cool but believe me they are all about making profits too. And they were worse to oversee because the people making them were often coked out and had no regard for anyone but the thrill of it all. But the worst part of the job was hiring the crews. These were people who lived from job to job and though several hundred dollars a day seems like a bunch of money they might only work two days a week. The owner of the company expected me to see his profits were protected by cutting the "best deal" I could with the crew. This meant squeezing their pay. I did not mind squeezing the owners of the stages we would rent, or squeezing the car rental companies, or the camera renting companies but I sure disliked getting technical workers down to what the owner expected to pay them. So here I was in double jeopardy. The owner was making a profit off my work and he expected me to make him a greater profit off other people's work. What a rat business that was.

JEN ANGEL: I don't like doing temp work a lot because people treat you like shit. Really, they do. If you're there for more than a couple of days, like if you're there for a few months, then you get left out of meetings, your long-term input isn't valued, any rewards are reserved for "real" employees. Temping really lets you interact with a lot of different kinds of people, so I feel like now I'm a good judge of people, especially managers, because I've had good and bad ones. There are some people who every comment out of their mouth makes you feel like shit, when if they rephrased they would just be giving you constructive criticism. Anyway, I had a long-term temp job recently at an engineering firm. The people were okay, except the office manager had some issues. She could be really good to you, but she had a couple of things that she just came down on you all the time for. She insisted that you be there at exactly 8:00 AM working at your desk. If you were 2 minutes late, she was all over you. And it's not as if it would matter —the engineers could have cared less if the secretaries were in their chairs at 8.00 AM on the nose. It was really annoying—to be polite—and I lost a lot of respect for her over her inability to see the bigger picture. I had the worst experience at that firm. I temped there for 5 months with the expectation of being hired. I was obviously doing good work for them and was well-liked by the staff. I developed a new database for them to use, was the most knowledgeable person on staff for certain computer programs, and overall proved myself to be an asset—worth much more than they were paying. When my conditional period as a temp was over, the office manager came to me and said they wanted to hire me on but she wasn't sure that they would be able to give me what I was making from the temp agency. I was so shocked I didn't know what to say. She was like: We might be only able to hire you on at $9.75 per hour, not $10.00. Since the company would be saving the fee that they were paying the temp agency, most temps expect to get the same if not more than what they had been paid as a temp. It was so lame. Sure it's only $.25, but over a year that adds up to over $500. Anyway, since I live paycheck to paycheck, and the job market is so poor here, what did she expect me to do, say no so that I could spend 6 weeks looking for another crappy job? She knew it, too. I ended up quitting to got to a new job a couple weeks after they hired me on permanent, mostly because I felt they had disrespected me and my abilities.

SANDER HICKS: I guess my worst job was working as a stock boy in aisle 5 of the F&M Drugstore over the summer of 1991. Mostly because my life in Virginia had come to an end, I was about to transfer schools and go to New York's New School, and I couldn't get out fast enough. The Gulf War had slaughtered all of those Iraqi soldiers and civilians, my first girlfriend had dropped out of school, and I was stuck putting chemicals and cleansers and air fresheners up on the shelves of the aisle in a big discount drugstore. And the worst aspects of the job were the muzak. They had made a tape loop of the stupidist AM radio schmaltz...obviously stuff that they could license for real cheap. Stuff like: Sherrrreerrieee-Sheery BABY....or the one about the guy who is poor and enters a drag strip race to raise money to buy his baby a ring, and then he dies in a crash singing Tell Laura I Love Her...or the song that goes My LIIIIIFFFEEE is such MISERY AND PAIN I Think I'll Never love again. Anyway, those songs are not all bad, and I obviously related to the ones I remember so well. But the same songs 20 times a day over your head is pure torture. In those days, I set up a space for myself in the back yard, in an old red shack in our yard. I would go back there at the end of the day, full of bile and confusion and air fresheners, plug in my guitar and microphone amps and scream, and sing, and make up songs. I made up a whole bunch of songs that summed up that summer—a tape called The CIA Pumps Soft Rock Into My Job.

RACHEL MORIELLO: The worst job had to have been driving the SCABS to and from their secret strike training. I really needed the money and the pay was good but I felt so bad about what I was taking part in! The people were the sleaziest, lamest people in the world. I was hit on and shit on daily...not to mention the fact that I had never driven in the city before—EVER—and there I was driving a huge van during rush hour. I was a nervous wreck. I actually got into an accident one morning. It was raining and I was on my way to pick them up. A car stopped short in front of me and I rear-ended that one and then smashed into a double-parked car on the side of the street. It was a gypsy cab and the owner of it came out of the building where he was (thankfully he wasn't in the car!) and he freaked out on me, threatening my life. When I went back to my employers to tell them, they didn't even ask if I was okay. They screamed at me and wanted to know how the van was.

GARY BADDELEY: My worst job was probably delivering newspapers in a small town in Australia—the kind where dogs really do chase you.

CHAZ MENA: Steve's Ice Cream Shoppe in Coconut Grove in Florida. This is the worst job that I ever had. The boss would smoke pot in the back (and never share with me) and scream out orders all day long: "Where's the 5-gallon sherbet?" "Don't answer the phone like that!" "You're serving too much ice cream!" "Remember to weigh each serving!" etc. One day I screamed back, "Fuck you, man!" and walked out in the middle of my shift. Good ice cream though, at Steve's.

REAL

JEN ANGEL: The first real nine-to-five type job (though it's actually 8 to 5 now since they couldn't possibly pay you for the lunch hour) I had was a couple of years ago—probably three years—I worked at a company called Steris in Mentor Ohio. It was my first 40-hour a week job (I was about 23 or 24 at the time), the first one with insurance, a dress code, etc. It was very corporate. I still have clothes from that time that I haven't worn since. The atmosphere was okay, I mean the people that I worked with on a day to day basis were nice (even if they were obsessed with TV shows and everyone with kids couldn't stop talking about Disney). But I was so bored. Even now, thinking about it, I can't figure out what exactly I was supposed to be doing or how I was supposed to be spending my time. It was very difficult for me to get there on time every day—why should I rush there just to sit at my desk and be bored? Of course I spoke to my supervisor about how they weren't "using my talents" or "challenging me" but nothing happened. I worked there 6 or 8 months, until I had had enough and decided to quit. They told me that they were just about to move me into a different section where I would have more engaging work, but really I feel like they were only saying that, or that they did mean it but it would have taken 6 more months to come through.

RACHEL MORIELLO: My first "real" job...hmm...have I had one? I guess you could say my only "real" job has also been my most rewarding: teaching artist. It has, for the most part, been a great thing in my life. When I started out I was doing in-school residencies (self-esteem building and communication skills through theatre) in Brooklyn and Queens—as far out as you could possibly go: taking the train to the last stop and then taking the bus, that kind of thing. I loved the work but I HATED the commute, so eventually I stopped taking those jobs and concentrated on Manhattan exclusively, unless it was a short residency or the pay was really good. Now I do mostly after-school programs, teaching acting and basic theatre skills. I also do residencies in-school for violence/drug prevention, that sort of thing.

CHAZ MENA: Only my acting work gets called a "real job." I guess what you mean is a job that is more mainstream: teaching acting at a high school of the performing arts—a "fame" school—in downtown Miami. This was a great place to work in, and I miss it dearly. This is the one thing I miss about Miami. My students enjoyed my classes and the faculty and the dean thought valued my contribution. The faculty also had an acting troupe that would put on plays twice a year. My teaching position lent me certain legitimacy in the eyes of my friends and family (who have always supported me). I miss teaching and have decided to become certified to teach in New York State.

JASON KUCSMA: I'm not sure I've actually had a "real" job. It's interesting, because I've been working some job or another since I was 14. I started out sweeping floors in a factory that a friend of my parents' managed. I also worked in a lumberyard for a number of years in high school. While I was in college, my parents insisted that I didn't have to work. They wanted me to focus on my studies, but I found that I needed to work in order to keep myself motivated and organized.

You work nine-to-five and somehow you survive till the night.
—BRUCE SPRINGSTEEN

EVERYTHING IN-BETWEEN

RACHEL MORIELLO: I have done just about everything to make a buck in this town. I have been a waitress, a bartender, and a caterer. I have worked as a receptionist, a promotional model handing out free samples and flyers on the street, I have been a teaching artist, a babysitter, a nude model; I have stuffed envelopes, cleaned toilets, and watched people having sex—all to keep my dream alive.

CHRISTINA MOSES: Well I have worked all over the place in many different fields. I am so young and have worked so many places. So far the jobs have been to support myself through high school and college.

RACHEL F.: Many theatre people worked as waiters to support their auditioning. I did not have a thick enough hide at the time to be able to do that well. Among the jobs I did were house painting, house cleaning, and interviewing people on the telephone for their political opinions for the Harris Polls. The priorities were to avoid working full time and/or to have flexible work hours. This would allow me to go to auditions. An acquaintance who was financial controller of an architectural firm allowed me to work part-time in his office, where I learned basic bookkeeping and computer skills. But when financial pressure arose from insufficient income from these part-time jobs, I found myself applying for full-time bookkeeping and accounting positions. I assured myself that such a job would not be permanent. After six months in a small real estate management company, I had learned all of the bookkeeping there and was bored. I moved to the accounting department of a medium-sized corporate law firm. Still, I was telling myself it would only be temporary. I was about 20.

GEORGIA GIANNIKOURIS: I was lucky enough to get a job at a diagnostic center that had barely even opened up. At that point I would have done anything! It ended up being an excellent experience. I worked with my closest friend and we had some incredible memories there. We were being paid well enough, and I was able to do just about anything I wanted. I made my own hours, I was only a part timer, and I loved my patients. I was able to help people there. NOTHING is more exhilarating and WHOLLY fulfilling as that. I repeat, I love people. All people. And I have the biggest desire to help anywhere I can. I'm very serious about that, and I would give up anything to do that. So, I felt good about working there. It wasn't like working in any office. I'd literally sit and listen to people's stories for long periods of time. Geez, I still call some of my patients to see how they're doing. We switched from suits, to scrubs, to suits with lab coats and nametags there. But I'm a student, so none of this was a career—it was part-time work. So, while I LOVED it, some of my co-workers were miserable. The problem eventually became that it was not fulfilling enough. I felt like my whole creative side needed some sort of quenching. I wanted a job that had something to do with my *passions*. As soon as I quit, I was broke, and I had to go back to asking my parents for money which I really don't like to do. Yet, I had this determination to do something I would love.

JASON KUCSMA: I've had a number of different jobs in the last five years. Some of them were average jobs as a night guard at the university and delivering sandwiches for a local restaurant. I've also worked for an extended amount of time (on and off) at my current place of employment. It's a nice locally-owned copy shop that does a lot of work for the university.

CHRISTINE HAMM: I saw the ad in the *Times* for an Administrative Assistant and sent in my resume. The good thing about a Master's in English; it can help you type and spell. My boss, a charming, animated man, interviewed me and we hit it off right away. Although I knew it was the corporate office of a church, he didn't mention any necessary religious affiliation, nor did he say that he would be out of the office most of the time. I was hired immediately. Day 1 was my orientation in human resources. "You must arrive at exactly 8:45 AM. Being one minute late more than five times in the first six months is grounds for disciplinary action.

You are allowed one ten minute break before lunch. This break must be taken no sooner than one hour after you arrive and no later than one hour before lunch. Lunch can only be taken between the hours of 12 and 2. It is exactly 45 minutes. You are allowed one ten-minute break in the afternoon. It must be taken no sooner than one hour after lunch, and no later than one hour before the end of the day. You must clock out at exactly 4:30 PM. You must be out of the office building by 4:45. All doors will be locked by then. Welcome to the largest administrative office of the Methodist Church. We hope you will enjoy working for us."

SUSANA SANTIZO: I used to bartend. This was definitely the worst job. I had to smile at greasy old men just so I could pay rent. I hate being phony especially for money. Four thousand shots and five thousand dollars later, I was out!

MANNY SIVERIO: I've been a gym floor instructor at various major New York health clubs. Doing more than just instructing people on fitness. There was a lot of other non-training chores I was responsible for primarily the cleaning and upkeep of fitness equipment. I moved up to being a gym floor manager, a gym service supervisor, and then an area Service Supervisor. Eventually, I moved onto training people privately in one-on-one training in both martial arts and fitness.

A.D. NAUMAN: I tried lining up jobs through temp agencies. Temp agencies, of course, automatically herd all young women into the typing test room. I'd never taken a formal typing course—I so dreaded being forced someday to work as a secretary. I'd taught myself how to type writing novels on my Mom's typewriter when I was in the eighth grade. What I was not able to do (and still can't) is look at someone else's draft, rather than at the keyboard, while typing. At first at these temp agencies, my typing speed was not fast enough. But after taking enough tests, I had the test sheet memorized, so I could look at the keyboard. After my 3-week eternity at the Association of Municipal Finance Officers, and several more weeks of unemployment, I got a job as a phone solicitor. By that point, of course, I was answering any and all ads in the job section of the paper.

My family was beginning to worry about me. They'd always been supportive of my writing; but I think their idea was that I'd marry some nice young aspiring lawyer and not have to worry about earning a living. They had not imagined me mucking around in some dark city, on the brink of doing anything for money. The phone soliciting also lasted about 3 weeks—I had no aptitude for it. This particular phone soliciting was selling credit card insurance. During one call I made, the guy yelled at me to get a real job. My bosses—two overly enthusiastic young guys—tried to coach me on how to sell. I was supposed to just keep talking, not let the solicitee ask any questions, then say, "So I'll sign you up for blah, blah, blah," click. At this time I would have happily taken a job waitressing. Anything was better than phone soliciting. However, when I went to apply at a few places, I was informed that I did not have enough experience: my previous jobs at Hardees, Pizza Hut, and Mr. Steak simply weren't enough. So I went back to secretarial work, this time at the American Association of Dental Schools. This job was more tolerable, because my desk was way in the back of a long row of offices and no one saw me (thus, no need to look cheerful), my boss appreciated the fact that I was underemployed and tried to find more interesting things for me to do, and it was only part-time—so I was only half-demoralized. But still extremely poor, and still not working very well on my fiction. After a year of life like this, I felt that working mindless jobs and saving myself for my art was not, well, "working" for me. Mindlessness has a way of perpetuating itself after the workday. I needed more challenge and more respect. So I moved back to St. Louis, where I had gone to college and would still have contacts, to make a foray into journalism.

RUSS KICK: I've worked several retail jobs as an "associate." Funny thing is, I did find some bright spots in the wage slavery. I get a sense of satisfaction from a job well done, even if it is a shitty line of work. The camaraderie was also nice. I made friends, flirted a lot, and managed to have a good time more often than would be expected at 10 cents above minimum rage, while still managing to do a good job. Dealing with the general public (or, as I would say in my darker moments, the genital public) was enlightening. Some customers—oh, excuse me: guests—were incredibly nice; I would actually enjoy helping them. Other people were complete, flaming assholes, insulting and demanding to the point of lunacy. They'd blame me because certain items were sold out, or they'd get mad because I wasn't aware of the features, strengths, and drawbacks of every one of the 100,000+ items the store stocked.

MARTA RUSSELL: Once I took a job as a taxi driver. There were not many female drivers back then, much less a crip with a limp, but the manager of the cab company did not discriminate. He gave me a job. So for several months I spent my time helping little old ladies carry their groceries home, fending off drunks, and transporting rude businessmen from the airport to their various destinations. When I'd go back to the cab company lot to gas up I would endure the wolf whistles from other cabbies. "What's your name honey?" When they heard Russell they'd say, "Are you sure that's not Jane Russell?" Every bit of life in Los Angeles is invaded by the film industry.

CHAZ MENA: When I got to New York, I had to get an agent, but I couldn't get an agent without being in a show. Then I could invite an agent to come see. But how to get a show without an agent, you follow? Well, I decided to sell my sperm. I went to a sperm bank to apply for a job that would allow me to earn $50.00 a squirt. Guess what? I couldn't go through with it. My wife was in Miami and wasn't due to arrive in NYC for a couple of months, so I was due to masturbate—and did—but I couldn't do it professionally. I am an amateur, I guess.

CHRISTINE HAMM: On Day 20, the office manager calls me into her office. Her office is filled with beanie babies on miniature bicycles, smarmy religious plaques, and doilies, lots of doilies. I hope she is going to explain to me where all the post-it notes and staplers are located, and how exactly to fix the Xerox machine when it jams. I've already gotten tired of answering the phone with the obligatory three sentence greeting, and I'm especially sick of hearing the callers' standard "praise the Lord," or, "God bless" 16 times a day. But the office manager, a woman with little to no imagination—if I am to judge by her hairstyle—has her own agenda. She needs to talk to me about a distressing trend she has noticed lately, especially, a distressing fashion trend. Despite the fact that my tattoos are adequately covered, my piercings minimal, and my hair, though short, flattened into Julie Andrews-style conformity, the office manager does not like my looks. Anne Taylor and the Gap (major compromises on my part) do little to pacify her. In short, her problem rests with the fact that I wear pants. My long and soul-killing search for the perfect Methodist dress has begun. I start off with two criteria: floor-length and floral.

GEORGIA GIANNIKOURIS: I took an unpaid internship at *Jane* magazine. I worked the fashion closet. It was an interesting experience, but what intrigued me the most was that I felt like somehow I was closer to the stars featured in the magazine. I got to go on a few photo shoots and help dress the models, as well, and I even bundled up the wardrobes that would go on major stars in L.A. Man, I felt like if I rubbed the clothes on me I'd be a step closer to them! I was fascinated by it! I would dress in my most stylish outfits (although I was warned to wear sneakers and comfortable clothes), just to feel like I was one of them. I'd be sitting there doing plenty of not-so-glamorous work, like packaging items into huge heavy body bags and dragging them down hallways and elevators ten times a day, (and I did this in heels) and I'd be so psyched! By the end of the day my feet were ready to fall off and I would want to collapse. One day the fashion stylists used me as their model to test different outfits and my eyes were glowing. Anytime I would walk by Jane or say two words to her I was like, "WOW!" It was as if maybe she'd let me write for her magazine or give me real work. Then came that dark cloud over me. Dissatisfaction. After all, I was doing all this for free, while these beautiful people were living their dreams. I never forgot something one model told me. She was a very pretty Asian girl who had a degree in biology, but was now modeling for money. She said that she felt so bored with what she was doing, and felt so dumb in a sense. Here she was, sitting pretty while people dressed her. It was a waste of brains. Another memorable thing was when a stylist said that she dressed people pretty for a living for one picture in a magazine that people probably wipe their butts with. It wasn't fulfilling for her either. Before I even got to make my decision to leave, Sept. 11th happened and that was that.

INDIO: I opened my own glass store in Harlem 'n started to sell 'n use drugs. I had four children but started havin' problems with my wife 'n we became separated. In 1973, I went to the federal prison in Danbury, Connecticut 'n took up some college courses 'n actin'. I came out in 1975 'n tried to get back with my wife to no avail. So, I moved down to 45th Street 'n went back to sellin' drugs, became a player with the ladies. Had 10-12 ladies that I took care of 'n they took care of me while I worked at Citibank.

PAMELA RICE: From a low-level book designer at a third-rate publisher in Chicago, I was promoted to production manager. Suddenly, I was responsible for a budget of about $500,000 a year. I had to make decisions. I had to take responsibility. I was a big fish in a little pond. It felt comfortable to me, but the pay was ridiculously low. After seven years of getting experience at the expense of pay, what do you know—I got downsized.

SETH ASHER: From late 1987 through 1990, then already a full-fledged CPA, I worked at Deloitte & Touche, a Big 6 international accounting firm that eventually sponsored my MBA studies at Columbia Business School. This was considered quite a perk and was handed out very selectively. The job and culture, however, were horribly insufferable. I had no real interest in business school, aside from the escape from work and some still persisting drive to get ahead.

A.D. NAUMAN: When I was in college, at Washington University (in St. Louis), I was editor-in-chief of the student newspaper. That was no small deal: we published twice a week, which is a lot for a student paper. The St. Louis journalism community had some small degree of respect for Wash University students with experience on the student paper, and I became a stringer for three weeklies: *The St. Louis Business Journal, The River Front Times*, and *The Rehabber*. Imagine my euphoria, after being a phone solicitor and a secretary, at being called "a writer." I regained some confidence. The work was not full-time but that, of course, was my plan. I needed all the extra time for writing fiction. Well, after about a week of being a stringer I remembered why I wasn't seriously pursuing journalism in the first place. Fiction writers do not necessarily make good journalists. I hate limiting myself to things that really happened. I kept wanting to make up facts and events and sneak them in, here and there. Plus, the articles I was being assigned were stupid and irrelevant—I have a pretty low tolerance for stupidity and irrelevance. My first assignments from *The Rehabber*, a paper for rich professionals fixing up their stately St. Louis homes, included an interview with a tuckpointer and a special feature on ceiling fans. *The Business Journal* had me doing something how businessmen can insure their insurance. *The River Front Times*, a weekly alternative paper, held more promise for generating interesting stories. I was given a few interviews to do with local politicians running for minor offices. Once again I felt irritated by the constraints of journalism—by having to be objective. So, I wasn't objective. The *Times* editor didn't appreciate this, spent several hours telling me how bad my articles were, made a long dramatic gesture-filled speech about how he'd have to rewrite the articles himself, and demoted me to calendar editor. Though, every now and then, I got to write articles for the advertising supplements. In the meantime, I was still broke, still working but not well on the fiction.

MICKEY Z.: I was employed many years ago by the Port Authority and worked picking up garbage at LaGuardia Airport. Yes, I actually was one of those hapless souls that everyone has a field day making fun of—carrying a red canvas bag and a long pole with a pointy jabber at the end to stab the debris I encountered. What made is intolerable was cleaning up the taxi stands. I worked out near the old Eastern Shuttle (which soon became the Trump Shuttle and I'm not sure what it's called today. Delta, maybe?). There was a massive taxi stand where the drivers could park their yellow death machines and wait like covetous vultures for the planes to land so they could prey on gullible tourists. As I strolled around picking up their toxic refuse, I'd observe the cabbies in action like a modern-day Margaret Mead. Almost to a man, the cabbies dined on putrid-smelling and unhealthy food. Every now and then, one of them would casually get out of his cab, unzip his pants, and simply whip it out to take a piss—letting loose a stream of liquid that would rival the Boston Harbor for health hazards. Trust me, you'd have to go pretty damn far to find a more abominable sight than what would happen next: Without skipping a beat, the cabbie would shake himself dry and hastily use the same hand to shovel a jelly donut into his mouth, making sure to lick the powdered sugar from those fingers. The worst part of all (yes, it actually gets worse) was the portable bathroom LaGuardia Airport provided for the drivers. Once the undersized booth got slightly dirty, the cabbies would start relieving themselves outside of it—*in public*—on a pile of old newspapers. Now, don't get me wrong, the idea of literally taking a dump on the *New York Times* has more than its share of merits, but this was not a political statement, my friends. Not by a long shot. Then, the next taxi driver to come along would impassively add to the burgeoning rankness with his own Burger King-inspired bowel movement. Needless to say, yours truly never went anywhere near this Superfund Site and I almost ended up in a fistfight with my boss when he demanded that I clean it up. Fortunately, my reputation as a martial artist preceded me and that Port Authority lifer chose discretion over valor.

PANAYIOTA PHAROS: I worked for a dating service. I literally sold sex legally to men and women. Basically, it is an intricate telephone dating service that requires people to record their personal ad in a category. It depended on whether you wanted a serious relationship, make some friends, or basically find someone to fuck. But in order for men to retrieve messages from women and interact with them in any way, they had to purchase a block of time which will be used towards messages and other paid features. Almost like buying a phone card and being allotted a certain amount of time to use as you please until it runs out and you have to buy another one. I've seen and heard everything! My first week there, listening to the ads on the system (we had to screen them for content), I couldn't believe what I was hearing. Men and women looking for dominant or submissive partners ("who's looking for daddy?"), wanting to worship women's feet, get watched while masturbating, watching women masturbate, wanting to get beaten till they bleed or having their asses spanked with mayonnaise and cold cuts………*hello!* Luckily, my job was only to provide customer service (the system was intricate—people had problems locating messages or not knowing how to set up their voicemail boxes, etc.), to sell the system to customers, and edit the ads going through. Sometimes though, men would get confused and think "customer service" meant something else. And when that happened, I'd have to tell them in the most professional and courteous manner that I would have to terminate the call unless they stopped "banging their cocks against the phone"—no other job in the history of legal employment would I ever get away with saying something like that! It was great fun and it definitely helped with my acting, as strange as it sounds. I got so used to hearing that type of language that it made me comfortable hearing about sex-related topics. So if I had to do a scene or a monologue that was especially explicit (even something like "The Vagina Monologues"), I would read through it like I was reading the Business section of *The New York Times*. Definitely made me more open-minded and comfortable with it as a whole. Also I never realized how afraid people are to talk about sex—even if they're in character! I used to be that way too—very embarrassed even only with the implication of sex! Selling sex changes a person though. Luckily for me the change was a positive one! Ha! Who would've thought???

JEN ANGEL: The most out-of-character job I had was as a nude model for art students at the art school in Columbus, Ohio. It didn't pay very well; I don't know why I was doing it. I also don't think it was daring or risqué. It was actually kind of boring.

RUSS KICK: It was interesting to experience different management styles. Some supervisors were pains, and I remember one manager who needed a high colonic. But then you had the supervisors who would ask, rather than tell, me to do things. I'd practically forget that they were my so-called superiors. It's like I *wanted* to help them. And this wasn't some mindfuck, either, but their real personalities, as I learned eating lunch with them, talking about personal (not too personal) matters, etc. I always resented the way employees were pitted against each other. I was asked twice to rat out fellow workers who had violated some little rule. I refused both times, and the managers quickly let it drop. At one store, we earned points—redeemable for various products—for every month that no employee was injured. If someone was hurt badly enough to miss time or require treatment, the points for the month would be erased and would start building again from zero. One day at work, we found out that a pregnant employee, in a previous shift, had been clobbered by a box that fell from a top shelf. Everyone was incredibly concerned... about whether that month's points would be erased. No one asked about the woman or the baby she was carrying. By the time I quit, I had enough points to buy something "really nice," like a CD player, but I refused to use the points from a system designed to ostracize people who get injured on the job.

CHRISTINE HAMM: Omigod, it's Day 35 and my job is so boring. All I have to do is answer the phone and receive and ship out book and CD orders. The phone rings about once an hour, and an order comes in about once a week. I haven't seen my boss for so long I've forgotten what he looks like. I wish I could use the free time to sketch, but my desk abuts the office of the office manager and I don't even have one cubicle wall. I've surfed the net till I'm blind, instant messaged all my friends five times, started 3 online journals and joined 15 Yahoo painting and writing clubs. And it's not even time for lunch yet. I'm on my fifth cup of coffee and I can still barely keep my eyes open. Someone's going to notice me nodding and think I'm a junkie. I suddenly remember that there's a couch in the woman's lounge on the 4th floor. Hardly anyone works on the 4th floor. I decide to take a little nap. On Day 45, my co-worker, a fellow secretary with a surfeit of plastic angels on her desk, urges me to go to the monthly all-staff prayer meeting in the chapel downstairs. She keeps reminding me that there's a free breakfast afterwards. Her insistent, probing questions about my religious background grate on me like an unwanted tongue in my mouth at the end of a date. I blurt out a (fantastic and untrue) statement that will come to haunt me later: "Actually, I'm a Buddhist." My coworker's mouth drops open and she backs away. In a few days, the whispers and stares begin. Soon, no one will even say good morning to me. On Day 62, I call in sick. I'm on the pill, and it's making me nauseous. Actually, the thought of work is making me nauseous. It's gotten so that I nap through lunch every day, and take a half-hour "nap-break" every day. This is the seventh time I've called in sick since I've started. I'm holding my breath as I wait for the disciplinary action. Holding my breath also makes me nauseous.

GREG RAPAPORT: I worked as a carpenter for 10 years during the late 80's and early 90's. I made some pretty decent cash back then. My boss was a great guy and the crew I was on always kept me on my toes physically and mentally. Drugs, of course, were rampant through the early part of my career as a carpenter, especially cocaine and weed. At that point, I had cleaned myself up so I enjoyed watching everybody else act like idiots for once.

PAMELA RICE: They say that being let go from a job can be the best thing to happen. After being restructured out of a job in Chicago, I came to New York to try to make it in the book publishing world. I bounced around a lot there, eventually being bounced out. Later, as a sales rep, I learned valuable interpersonal skills, but the "b.s." I had to dish out eventually rubbed me the wrong way. From there, I got into computer graphic design, eventually offering my services as a freelancer.

SPARROW: I worked as a house painter at the Place Apartments, a modern decadent apartment complex for University of Florida students, with a swimming pool. My friend Michael worked with me, and we had long confidential conversations, and also useful silences. After that I worked for three years at Mother Earth, a natural food store in Gainesville. I bagged dates and cashews and raisins and almonds; also I ordered the herbs, and sometimes worked the cash register. This was a satisfying, idealist, friendly, awfully amusing job. Once, while visiting friends in Bozeman, Montana (1976), I answered an ad for a job unloading carpets. There was a carpet auction at a Holiday Inn, and me and a large guy had to hold up carpets for the bidders. I wasn't strong enough, and the other guy (with a mixture of pride and annoyance) did most of the work. Twice I was a migrant farm worker. I picked cherries outside Bellingham, Washington with four other guys from the Rainbow Gathering, for four days in 1976. We made just enough money to buy dinner every night—plus we ate lots of cherries (which were ripe, and covered with pesticides). Also in Cheltenham, England, in The Cotswolds, my wife and I picked apples and plums for two weeks (1986). I had to climb a ladder forty feet high, to capture the last few plums on a towering tree. (We started late in the harvest.) Again we made enough money to buy dinner. Three times I was a telephone solicitor (now the term is "telemarketer"): while visiting Austin, Texas, I worked for a liberal political candidate, calling up voters (for three days); I tried to lure Coloradans to subscribe to *The Rocky Mountain News* for four months in Denver; and I did "marketing research" in New York City— across from the Empire State Building—for three months. This last job was humiliating. "I just have a short survey," I was trained to say—and 20 minutes later, most respondents would lose patience. (I had lied.) Also sometimes we had to call up air freight companies and ask their rates, over and over. These rates were secret, but we were working for their competitors, trying to sniff out the answers. "You just called five minutes ago asking about a package from Seattle to Des Moines!" the clerk would shout, hanging up. The woman next to me could imitate an Asian accent perfectly, and never had a problem.

A.D. NAUMAN: I began to think that starving for my art wasn't necessarily the best thing for my art. Apparently, some people can do it. I couldn't. I needed more stability. I needed to be not impoverished and constantly frantic about where the next paycheck was coming from. I needed to find work that I half enjoyed and was decent at. So, after four months of stringing, I applied for and got a job at a medical publishing company: the only publishing company in St. Louis—the C.V. Mosby Company—and entered the world of cubicles.

SUSANA SANTIZO: I have to admit I am guilty of pursuing the "dirty green." I am one of six so it's safe to say money didn't grow on trees in my house. Once I turned thirteen I was able to help my parents, paying for my clothes, sneakers, and extras. The more I make the more I could help even till today. I will stay conscious of my morals and values, but my family comes first. If I have to do something degrading to save my mother from stretching her pennies I'll do it, if I don't I'll be a sell-out. In other words, I can't say I've had a sell-out job because I never sold out.

MANNY SIVERIO: I've written for such magazines as *Black Belt*, *Inside Karate*, *Kick Illustrated*, *Inside Kung Fu*, *Karate Illustrated*, *Fighting Stars*, *Official Karate*, *Martial Arts Training*, *Karate International*, and *Combat Karate*.

CHRISTINA MOSES: I have worked at the GAP (oops!), a woman's gift basket company out of her home, Urban Outfitters. I was a P.A. on the film *The Negotiator*, a real estate agent's personal assistant, a hostess, and cocktail waitress.

MARTA RUSSELL: I worked for the Walt Disney Corporation for about a year and a half on the film *Tron*. The studio was walled in on all sides, high security and one had to have a pass to get on the lot. Disney Corp called me (and the other workers) an "independent contractor" and set me up in a trailer off one of the main buildings on Mickey Mouse lane (or was it Dopey Lane?). Later I learned that I wasn't really an "independent contractor" because I used Disney's tools, Disney's camera, Disney's light boxes, Disney's camera sheets, and I brought none of my own tools to work. It was a moneymaking move on Disney's part to set up a whole crew for the film without the extra expense of paying benefits.

That way they did not have to pay any Social Security, or disability insurance or take out any federal income tax. Disney saved on labor costs in other ways too. All the ink and paint matte work was shipped to Taiwan where laborers there worked around the clock at much cheaper rates than American union ink and paint workers would have to paint those mattes. And they worked under worse conditions. One of the art directors remarked to me that some of the workers would sleep on their desks over there. That was what is now called globalization really an extension of imperialism, though at the time I was just an artist and did not know what was really going on. At the time all I knew was that it left a bad taste in my mouth—later I realized how all of us were exploited.

TIM WISE: After Duke fizzled in 1992, I found myself in a tough spot. No work, no money, and still considered too young and inexperienced by most of the non-profits I was trying to find work with. Or there was no work to be had, especially in New Orleans. So I was considering going back to grad school, as was my girlfriend at the time. Thankfully we both bombed the GRE and got rejected from everywhere we applied. I say thankfully because within a few years things would turn around for me, and if I had been in academia, getting a Ph.D., I wouldn't be doing what I'm doing now. But back then, man, I didn't know what I was going to do. First I sold my baseball card collection, which I had coveted since my youth. And it was a damned nice collection too: I'm talking cards worth probably $30,000 in all, but which I sold for so little, that I can't even bring myself to admit it. It was pathetic. But it allowed me to pay my bills for a few months. Then I took a job for a few months stocking wine racks at a New Orleans gourmet shop and wine store. Fancy wine, fancy food, and lots of fancy asshole customers who naturally looked down on the "stock boys." Wine people are a sad lot: they really think their knowledge of fine wine makes them special people. Jesus. Oh well, at least I know which bottles to steal come the revolution. A little radical wine humor.

SETH ASHER: In 1991, now a CPA and MBA, I got a job with Merck Pharmaceuticals, which at first, seemed like a refuge: cushy job, nice pay, great benefits, job security, etc. The job initially served as a tonic in that it got me away from brutal Deloitte & Touche—where as public auditors we were little more than the confused outsiders trying to understand the accounting mess made by the corporate stooges who were our clients—and provided decent working conditions and superficially respectful treatment. However, over time I started to feel weary of the pathetic corporate lemming culture, the meaningless interactions and conversations with other workers, and the horrible asphaltscape of New Jersey. Eventually I started to also despise the company's obscene profit margins on drugs; the power trips of the executives; the obvious waste of money and resources the corporate bureaucracy represented; the driving of a car to work. However my years at Merck and prior years at Columbia Business School are probably when I started reading more avidly. I then had, for the first time in my life, enough time and initiative to explore many new ideas. Eventually, at Merck, I reached a point of utter desperation. I was despondent about getting up for work. Severe depression aptly describes my emotional state at the time. I felt hopeless, even suicidal. My wife Esther was no help. I was desperately trying to plan my way into recovery and needed a meaningful occupation. Esther emphasized the earning potential of any contemplated job change. One serious answer I was considering was becoming a schoolteacher. I also considered: natural/vegetarian café work, Kibbutz work, even studying Jewish philosophy to ultimately teach at a secular college. I got nothing but opposition from Esther for all of these ideas. Esther, as an investment banker, had been making several hundred thousand dollars per year (today that figure has climbed to new heights). She only wanted me to make a lot of money so that perhaps she could quit working at her dreadfully stressful job and still maintain a yuppie lifestyle. I left Merck to go work at American Express Financial Advisors. Months before lining up my new job I was so miserable I had to tell my boss. This is the same boss that hired me into a new and more desirable area of the company's financial organization and provided an early promotion and career boost. I explained my unhappiness and that I would need time to explore other career options. He actually put up with this scheme and my feeble job performance, funny enough.

MICKEY Z.: To deal with my Port Authority job, I had an astounding number of scams to get over and not actually do much work. Ultimately, I fell into a smooth routine that helped get through this summer ordeal without breaking a too much of sweat. Every morning, I'd report to work, climb into a giant yellow Port Authority bus, and get myself driven to my very own workstation conveniently located on the outer reaches of the airport. Once there, I'd stroll around and do some negligible cleaning before making a beeline for the Eastern Shuttle building. After hiding my conspicuous stick and bag, I'd buy two or three newspapers and enter the cafeteria to partake in an unhealthy breakfast. The next part of my diabolically uncomplicated contrivance was to locate a cafeteria table that effectively concealed my whereabouts. After some trial and error, I was able to select the ideal table. It was strategically located near an particularly enormous column so when anyone entered the cafeteria, the only way they'd see me was if they walked into the joint about twenty feet and specifically peered around the column to look. So, I'd consume my over-priced breakfast and read my newspapers to get my daily dose of corporate propaganda. Often, I'd lay my overloaded head on the table like a nursery school student and take a mini-nap if the mood possessed me. At noon, I'd awake and stagger out in the summer sun and catch the yellow bus back in to the main office where I could punch out for lunch. Since I lived so conveniently close to the airport, I'd drive home (still a motorist back then) to feast on a homemade lunch and wish my Mom luck as she'd leave to go take care of my grandfather for the afternoon. After stuffing my smirking face, I'd set my alarm for 2:30 P.M. and fall soundly asleep for the next two hours. When that alarm would ring, I'd scurry out to my car and drive the few blocks back into the employee parking lot to wait for the yellow bus to bring back those of my co-workers who actually earned their pay each day. As the bus emptied, I'd slip out of my car, mingle with the exhausted workers, dump my uniform in my locker, and punch out for the day. Then, I'd get back in the car and head home for the day. This scam lasted for a little more than two months. I ended up getting transferred. My bosses knew I was screwing up but they just couldn't ascertain how. They got their retribution by assigning me to the George Washington

Bridge to become a toll collector, but I quit that gig after a week and had the last laugh. No way was I going to inhale exhaust fumes for eight hours a day, five days a week. I get enough of that as a lifetime New Yorker.

RACHEL F.: Today so many offices have "smart casual" dress code—dressing down shows clout, that you don't need to impress anyone. But in a law firm in the 80's? No. You needed a jacket, skirt, a blouse of a non-stretch material, panty hose, and what I call secretary shoes. This I didn't like at all. I could not afford expensive business clothes, so my clothes were the wardrobe of a clerical worker–that's what I was. So the "trappings" I found very boring and conformity-inducing, although learning various tasks were interesting, and I liked many of the people I knew there. There was a woman who worked at the firm as a legal secretary. She was overweight, a chain-smoker, always looked disheveled, worn out and irritated, with circles under her eyes. She told me that she had gone to work there after graduating from acting school. She warned me that she had intended to stay for three months, but had been there for ten years. I took her caution very seriously.

A.D. NAUMAN: Within two weeks of starting the job at Mosby, at the age of twenty-three, I thought to myself, "My life is now officially over: I am dead and entombed in a cubicle." I recalled that, as a young child in school, I could not bear to be trapped in a school desk; at all times some part of my body had to be moving—a foot, a knee, my hands. And so it seemed I'd made yet another vocational mistake. On top of my growing horror of the cubicle, I made another awful discovery: though my salary of $11,000 a year was indeed vastly greater than the previous year's $4000, I was still quite broke. However, that job had some benefits. I did manage to stay there for two years, as opposed to my usual one to four months. First, Mosby had "flex time"—partly in compensation for the crummy salary. You had to work 8 hours a day but could start any time you liked before 9:30. Well, a late starting time is ideal for an insomniac writer. Better yet, no one kept track of your hours. Almost everyone else started at 7:30 and left at 3:30—

and then everyone was gone. So the derelict writers on staff started at 9:30 and left at 4:00. In my opinion, these are ideal work hours. The other great benefit was how many young people there were on staff—a whole slew of English majors striving to be fiction writers. There, I met the man I would later marry. We all took many breaks and long lunch hours. My co-workers were so much fun, by the end of the day my jaw would hurt from laughing so hard. If it sounds like we were primarily just goofing off, we were. My boss reprimanded me often for "chatting around" too much. (My boss was a very short woman with a bad bleach job and hips so wide they made her waddle. She was fortyish and unhappily married. She had a poster of Tom Selleck hanging on her office wall. One day she came in to work in a new suit and I realized she'd lost about 30 pounds. Shortly thereafter, she left her husband. However, she did not get remarried to Tom Selleck—at least as far as I know.)

SPARROW: None of my jobs have been terribly high paying. I was on TV once, in *The United States of Poetry* (a PBS special); for that I made six hundred dollars. Or was it four hundred dollars? Anyway it was one afternoon. That was the closest I have been to crime or lucrative money. (But I found it disturbing when they referred to me as "the talent.")

CHRISTINE HAMM: On Day 80, the disciplinary meeting commences in human resources. The head of HR points out that I've been over one minute late 27 times in the first three months. I try hard to care. I'm told that if I get a doctor's note they'll forgive all my absences. I call my doctor and call in sick for the rest of the week. This does not go over well. Day 95: I've managed not to fall asleep all day. I'm self-publishing a poetry chapbook using the PC on my desk and their Xerox machine. I'm having a problem printing the pages so I that I can staple them into book form. The whole facing page issue, when the page is 4 by 5 inches and printed in two columns and double sided, has me in a quandary. I've never been good at geometry. I waste two days and hundreds of sheets of paper before I'm able to put together 50 chapbooks. Every time someone comes into the

Xerox room where I'm cutting, coping and stapling I get as nervous as Cindy Crawford in a Twinkie factory. Luckily the axe never falls. No one ever looks at my work; no one cares about anyone else's work, or, most of the time, about their own. The invoices and book orders have started to pile up on my desk.

SANDER HICKS: When I first got to New York, I was so happy to be out of Virginia, everything about New York was fascinating and lush. And Kinko's on 12th Street was a lot like the Snack Bar at the pool—you were at the center of everything, there was a lot of action. Everyone used to come through that Kinko's. I met Lach, Roger Manning, John S. Hall, Lady Miss Kir from Dee Lite. David Byrne used to come in there, so did Matthew Modine. And it was a rush to work at Kinko's at times, especially when Johnny Stritehoff was key-op. There was a special language you had to learn to be a part of the shift, the calls and code words used to communicate the times needed to run certain jobs, communicate about the status of certain orders. There was a lot of paper flying around, stacks of copies and jobs, and boxes. You got the sense that you were part of a powerful machine, a big tank made of people and machines that could produce a lot of printed documents really fast. A Xerox 5090 can make 1000 copies in 7 minutes. Nobody was faster than John Stritehoff. He spun around the key-op area, jumping between three machines: 2 Xerox 5090s and a smaller 5100 for resumes and quicker, smaller jobs. He was a legend, and people used to come in just to watch him work. He was an odd one, because although he created his own myth, and acted in such a theatrical, big way, over time he would confide in me that he was feeling like a circus freak, he didn't like all the people staring at him. And he drank a lot, too much, every night after work we would go around the corner to the Cedar Tavern. Although it's a nice place, they welcomed us, since we worked around the corner. Stritehoff eventually was moved by Bagwell to a different store, and his weird psychic connection to the 12th Street store was broken, and his life unraveled. It's weird; you can't really move Stritehoff, Bagwell tried to force him to break out of his self-destructive habits by making him move to a slower store, but it didn't work. Stritehoff eventually quit and got work as a bar-back in a Columbia University area bar, a grubby place on Broadway called Canon's. I mean, it's a nice place for a college bar, but I resent it. I tried to get him to come work for me at Soft Skull, and it was great for a while, but then he started sleeping there, too, down in the basement in a spare room we had. Eventually he just up and quit on me, going to Florida and staying there last Christmas, 2000. When he came back to New York, he was homeless. He showed up at my door on Suffolk Street a couple days before I moved out. I had worked as the Super of these two buildings with their vast basements for 5 years, but I had gotten fired and was moving on. Stritehoff wanted to crash on the floor. He was without a place to stay, all of his stuff was stashed somewhere. This was early September 2001; I hadn't seen him since he left Soft Skull and me in mid December 2000. I reluctantly gave in and said he could spend one night on my floor. He was supposed to come back and meet me at 9 PM. later that night but he never showed. I guess the corollary to all of this Kinko's stuff is that Kinko's wasn't the best job I ever had. It was probably the worst, disguised to look like the best. Look at the way it ate people up. Look at Johnny Stritehoff, homeless on the streets of the city, or even look at Stuart Bagwell, once a poised and inspirational manager, who got fired by the company when they were rolling up all of their individual partnerships and becoming more of a corporate monolith. That really shattered Bagwell, and he never really recovered. Eventually he left the city to go back to school in South Carolina.

INDIO: I decided to get a new life 'n went to work at the American Indian Community House, went back to college 'n remarried. We had one child but drugs 'n her feeling for women caused us to get a divorce.

MANNY SIVERIO: When I working in nightclub security, I was usually the smallest bouncer on staff and the one most likely to be "tested" by a tough guy. I'm not a violent person by nature, but I'm also not physically imposing. I'd always try to defuse the situation and reason with the parties involved and I'd say this approach worked about 90 percent of the time. The other ten percent were not as fortunate. One night, I had to toss a guy out of the club. He didn't want to leave quietly, and I could see there was no talking my way out of this one. So, I decided to play a game of quick draw, you know, like the old gunfighters. I placed my hands at my sides and pushed my chin out towards him, offering him the first shot. As soon as this guy showed the tiniest hint of movement, I hit him with three consecutive punches and down he went. I wanted to finish him off but man, he started crying and I didn't have the heart to go any further. Right then and there, I knew I wasn't cut out for bouncing.

PANAYIOTA PHAROS: Well, my dating service job ended in January 2002 because the entire office closed and the customer service has been re-routed to their main operational center in Toronto, Canada. I was there for a year and half. In addition to that, I've been bartending for at this lounge in Astoria, Queens (where I live) and occasionally host poetry readings there too (which is awesome!).

A.D. NAUMAN: From my Mosby co-workers came a writing group, and by the end of my two years there, I was finally writing some worthwhile short stories. Looking back, I do think that the stability, though very very dull and still not lucrative, had a good impact on my writing. Though I still didn't have much money, I no longer had to worry about having none at all. I was able to establish a writing routine; I developed a strong writing habit which I've never really lost since, through subsequent times of instability. During those two unlikely years I became a lifelong writer; I knew I wasn't going to be one of those people who say they want to be a writer, then give up because it's too hard to integrate writing into a normal life. I knew then I'd be able to do it—to never give up. From that point on, lunch hours, evenings, weekends, and holidays were spent scribbling and typing, scribbling and retyping. I discovered that all the hard work needed to be supplemented by a willingness to steal from my employer: Xerox paper, typewriter ribbons, and especially time. After Mosby, I moved up, to a job that did pay well. It was a PR-ish kind of job at the Washington University Medical School. Though I moved up from the cubicle, being stuck all day in a little beige office was not much better. However, I had various responsibilities that took me out of the office. So I'd go breezing past the secretaries, announcing that I had a "meeting" to go to (they hated me); and I could disappear for long stretches of time, sit in the hospital cafeteria, and work on stories. Sometimes I actually would go to the meetings and pretend I was taking notes when I was writing a story. I stayed at that job a year and a half. The pay was high. I was living in low-rent St. Louis in the 1980s and I managed to save enough in that time to quit, take a 7-week trip to Europe, and from there go to graduate school. Unbeknownst to me, I had acquired enough experience in medical editing and writing to have created the all-important niche. For the next 6 years, I lived pretty comfortably as a graduate student/research assistant/medical abstractor.

RACHEL F.: It was a happy day when the law firm went out of business. That meant lots of free time for auditioning. When unemployment ran out, I joined the accounting headquarters of a "world-class" restaurant chain. I was the payables clerk for various restaurants. The owner was a total crook. He'd run up huge bills with food vendors, not pay them, then when the threats of lawsuits came due, negotiate settlements with the companies who didn't want the expense of the battle. Then he'd move on to the next vendor. Rumor had it that the restaurant industry had a bad reputation for this supposedly common practice. He'd have his wife managing the Beverly Hills restaurant, his girlfriend managing the Miami one–the whole scene really was enough to make you retch. I spent my days taking calls from vendors pleading for their money, which we'd pay out in small, late doses. We goofed off as much as we could–we were not particularly well managed–even our bosses treated the place as a bit of a joke. But one of my bosses, Jim, would come over to my cubicle and rest his chin on the top of the partition, and look down over the little wall to see what I was doing. I used to threaten to put glue on it, so he'd get stuck like that. Processing hundreds of invoices each day, I began working on an outline for a book, "Designing Invoices for Fast and Easy Payment–a Guide for Small Businesses." It was to be a colorful workbook, with lots of illustrations of good features, and software resources. I thought I could market it to the small business press and to software developers. There was plenty of time, space, and privacy to do all sorts of projects. One day I counted six hours of non-work on the job. My biggest side-project became my volunteer work. I became volunteer coordinator of a community garden in a local park. I wrote the newsletters at my job, made the calls, printed invitations to garden demonstrations and events I had organized. Meanwhile I had spent years of evenings rehearsing off and on for one amateur theatre production after another. I never pursued stock theatre, which would have earned me a union card, because I refused to leave New York City. I never pursued an agent, because I was prim about only doing serious theatre. I did not go about the business of building a theatre career in any sort of practical way at all. I was getting lots of amateur experience, and telling myself the future would take care of itself, and whatever happened, I would enjoy the process. I was, in fact, hiding.

RICHARD MILLER: From the kitchen gigs I moved onto landscaping; it's at this gig that I discovered the importance of getting paid off the books, don't pay taxes if you can avoid it. Chances are if you are cutting lawns your not making much cash anyhow. Why give a third to the government? So they can build bombs and guns when you have rent to pay? The thing about landscaping in upstate New York is that there is winter; this really puts a damper on things. Rather than counting on there being a lot of snow to shovel for cash, I took a job working construction. It was at this job that I learned the nuances of hammers, nails, and primal behavior. Working with bikers, ex-cons, and misfits, as you are likely to be doing on an upstate New York construction site is a great way to find your own base personal values. I worked relatively dangerous industrial jobs, so I had the necessary catalyst for a lot of ethical meditation, pulling nails and pouring cement can be a sort of Zen exercise. During these times, I was reading Hunter Thompson, William Burroughs, and Abbie Hoffman as well as listening to Bob Dylan, the Dead, and Frank Zappa. These influences combined with a healthy amount of recreational chemistry and an outsider's perspective could help anyone to better understand the structure of our society; as well as come up with creative sources of income. This is after all a capitalist Republik. Always remember bank accounts, credit cards, loans, etc. these are all chains which we place on ourselves. If we keep our lifestyles somewhat simple then almost any form of income will support us. It also sends a clear message of "hey fuck you" to the world, and that's an important thing to do. I believe that survival without succumbing to all the pressure out there is in itself a form of activism.

RUSS KICK: My shortest job lasted a couple of days. I was working the 4:00 PM-midnight shift for a (non-adult) bookstore in a seedy part of town. The second night some crazy fucker kept demanding money from me. He followed me to McDonald's on my lunch break. I gave him a few bucks, then quit the next day. I wasn't going through that shit for minimum wage and no benefits. The manager was furious; she thought I was overreacting, but I knew that place was trouble. It turns out that the weekend before I started, neo-Nazi skinheads had invaded the store and harassed the employees. Within a week of my quitting, a guy got shot while in the drive-through line at the Wendy's across the street from the bookstore. I'm sure the manager was able to hear the gunshots from the store. Here's your $3.75 an hour (after taxes), Mr. Kick, thank you for getting stalked and harassed, beaten down by skinheads, and capped in the head.

MICKEY Z.: I've performed in a dozen or so films (yes, I use that term loosely) starting with a Billy Blanks flick. Over the ensuing years, I did manage to move, well, laterally, I guess. All the movies I worked on were filmed in the metropolitan area so at least I got to sleep at home after toiling all day as a muscular, celluloid ghoul or drug dealer or security guard whatever. One oppressively warm New York City summer day in 1987, I got the call to "act" in yet another super-low-budget classic, *Robot Holocaust*. I had worked with the producers before: squished by a monster in *Breeders* and buried under two hours of special effects make-up as a zombie in *Necropolis: City of the Dead*. This time, me and my friend, Fast Eddie Mallia, had dual roles. We played "air slaves" and robots. As air slaves, we fought to the death and that's precisely why we were hired: we could fight and we looked good doing it in skimpy outfits. As robots, we were so thoroughly ensconced in rubber costumes, there was zero chance that any of the five people who actually ended up seeing *Robot Holocaust* would identify us as the loin-clothed gladiators who had just gotten zapped by a ray gun in the previous scene. The air slave fight scene was filmed inside the squalid Brooklyn Navy Yard with minimal crash padding. By the time we finished the scene (garnering a long round of applause, thank you), we were covered in both dirt and bruises. After considerable complaining, we gained access to the showers, unaware that the drains were clogged and the cats kept in the building to keep rats away appropriated those same showers as their kitty pan. Within minutes, Eddie and I were in ankle-deep water with cat droppings floating by. Back at the Navy Yard the next day, it was even hotter. The slightest motion initiated a gradual process of sweat drenching my frame. We donned the aforementioned rubber ensemble and there were problems:

-*The costumes allowed no air inside to get inside*
-*We had zero peripheral vision*
-*We had to scurry up and down stairs for several takes*
-*Eddie was required to wield a real sword*

The director, who I'm confident has since found a new vocation, bellowed at us to proceed faster and look "more imposing" as we negotiated the steps, a pool of perspiration trailing behind us. This provoked more grumbling and, when our scenes were wrapped, a very odd thing transpired. Both Fast Eddie and I had experienced the obligatory hassles getting paid for the prior work we had done for this company (and just about every company, for that matter). For *Robot Holocaust*, the producers cut us a check on the set. At that juncture, we ascertained we would not become part of their celluloid repertory company.

Postscript: Fast Eddie was the one of the very few friends who braved the teeming rain to hear me give a talk in Manhattan when *Saving Private Power: The Hidden History of "The Good War,"* came out 13 years after *Robot Holocaust* was filmed.

SPARROW: My wisest boss was Marco Polo Stefano, head gardener at Wave Hill, a botanic garden in the Riverdale section of the Bronx. I worked there the summers of '72 and '73. At that time I had no belief in horticulture, but I enjoyed the leisurely tasks—a lot of mulching and trimming wisteria—plus I worked with my good friend Harvey. Marco was humorous, aesthetic; he had worked at the Museum of Modern Art while Frank O'Hara was there. He had just begun shaping Wave Hill to his plan. Twenty-three years later I returned, and I saw the Taoist landscapes I had (in small part) contributed to—like Charles Mingus songs transformed into flowers!

SETH ASHER: American Express Financial Advisors offered me the eventual possibility of autonomous work; its potentially lucrative profits were appealing to Esther. For four and a half years I worked seventy hours or more weekly, sometimes in very humiliating situations. And at times the conditions were intolerable: under the close supervision of a domineering, control freak Vice President, or sharing an office with a malicious and pathological liar, or just the general culture of having to sell, sell, sell, sell, especially the products they emphasize using the propaganda they generate. And it seemed to me that I was the only one there that saw the ugliness of the sales culture; a voice in the wilderness. In August 1998, I opened a home office in my Brooklyn apartment and thereby cut out $35,000 of annual overhead (financial advisors are responsible for all of their expenses, including office, phone, computer, supplies, etc. which all must get covered by commissions). This greatly removed pressure from me. It allowed me to significantly ease up. Of course, the removal from that creepy office gave me a much healthier lifestyle.

A.D. NAUMAN: The discovery of medical abstracting is one of my greatest strokes of luck. (Though the doing of medical abstracting has nothing to do with luck.) I'd moved to Chicago, with the man I would eventually marry, who stumbled across the ad in the newspaper. A company called Year Book was hiring writers to write summaries of articles from medical journals that were collected into annual volumes and sold to doctors as an overview of the year's research. The articles were on every imaginable subspecialty: psychiatry, hand surgery, infectious diseases, gastrointestinal disorders, cancer, podiatry. The company did not pay per hour, they paid per piece: that meant the faster you worked, the more money per hour you'd make, and the more time you would have...to write. It was perfect for me. I'm a very fast worker. The key to being a fast worker is to not care that much about the work. Seriously, I've seen peers agonize over what details to put in these summaries. "Jesus Christ," I'd think, "just put something in and go on to the next one." I got faster and faster. Soon I was doing an enormous amount of abstracts per week, and I had time for everything: the work, my classes, and the fiction. I produced a vast amount of short stories and a novel. Several stories were published, and I found an agent to shop around my two novels. It was exactly the right balance of enough income, intellectual challenge, and time to write. As if that weren't heavenly enough, my boyfriend, also a fiction writer, had enrolled in the Writer's Program at the University of Illinois-Chicago and brought home an excellent circle of friends who became my second writing group. Those were the best years (ten years ago) it's too bad we never appreciate the best years at the time. It's too bad we can't choose to stay in a time, like we can choose to stay in a place.

TIM WISE: I worked as a research assistant for an economic journalist in New Orleans, researching international trade issues. I learned a lot, but hated it. Got paid like $200 a week I think. The guy I worked for is a big neo-liberal pundit now, with the Council on Foreign Relations. He very much enjoys—one might say covets—being a "mainstream" talking head and writer. Good for him, I guess. And also good for me that I got the hell out of that world. Not too long ago, I bumped into him in the restaurant of this wonderful hotel in Duluth, Minnesota. He was in town for a speech and so was I, and we were both staying there I guess. I said hello, and he was a total asshole to me: acted like he didn't remember who in the hell I was. Of course, to me I found it funny because here he was, a mainstream commentator, and here I was, a radical activist and commentator, and we're both eating the same entree, at the same hotel, and both being brought in for speeches. So it told me that one doesn't have to kiss the ass of powerful people or become a member of the punditocracy in order to be taken seriously, or to get to consume some damned good crème brulée along with some of that fancy-ass wine. After the research gig, I did a couple of months lobbying for a Tax Justice group in Baton Rouge, then was unemployed again so I took a position setting up seasonal displays at a mall, where my girlfriend was working as event coordinator. I actually helped stage a fashion show for God's sake: with some damned mall fashions, which was a trip for sure. That lasted about three months, and then I was back to politics, working as a grant-writer (and a bad one at that) for the Louisiana Injured Worker's Union. I was getting $150 a week for that one, plus a portion of any money I raised, which was next to nothing.

RACHEL F.: I was in the chorus of an established amateur opera company in Brooklyn, when I got the idea to place an ad for a gardening service in their program. I designed the ad at my job. Calls came in and I began weekend work in the springs and summers, learning on the job, reading up on whatever I needed to know. I also had some freelance bookkeeping jobs–a lawyer from the previous law firm hired me to visit once a month to do his bookkeeping, and recommended me to some of his acquaintances. So here I was involved in all of these other things: rehearsing, gardening, freelance bookkeeping, when the restaurant headquarters was running into serious financial problems. Also, I had developed some serious health problems as a result of always running around to rehearsals. I was chronically sleep-deprived and ate a fairly poor diet, though I didn't know it at the time. Chronic bronchitis had caused chronic asthma. My employer also refused to provide me with a smoke-free environment. I did some major reevaluations. I wanted a better balance, and some of the early motivations that had led me to theatre had dried up. In my youth, the choice had felt like a life or death issue; I believed that I needed to do theatre for some sort of emotional survival. Now theatre was something I was trained in and enjoyed, but did not need to do. It was only one of numerous tools I could make use of, in any number of ways or settings. I applied for, and was accepted into, a liberal arts undergraduate program at a university that appealed to me very much. Amidst the talk of reducing operations at my job, I asked my boss to lay me off. He said no. I began doing only the bare basics, slowing everything else down. He acquiesced. I used the wonderful time that followed to begin school part-time, and to build up my freelance bookkeeping service. I loved school at the two-evenings-a-week pace, and my new business flourished. I set my own work-hours, and chose my clients. My ideal formula was: one-third school, one-third work, and one-third play (leisure, slowing down, learning how to take care of my health). I loved the autonomy and flexibility.

RUSS KICK: I also worked construction for a week a few years ago. I almost had a heat stroke: green dots exploding in front of my eyes, getting chills and goose bumps in 95-degree heat. It isn't worth dying or getting brain damage, no matter how badly I needed the money, I quickly decided. Interesting thing was: the construction company, which was quite small, only had two teams. One was a rough and tumble bunch, with one guy who had just gotten out of prison. The other group was Christian guys, mainly family men. I worked with both teams, and let me tell you, the troublemakers were by far my favorites. They were nice, easygoing, and funny as hell. The guy who had been in the joint was the best of them all. The guys in the other group were petty, homophobic, macho pricks with something to prove. I loathed every minute with them.

CHRISTINE HAMM: On Day 116, my boss is back. He knows I'm frustrated, and asks me how my paintings are going. I show him some samples of CD and book covers I've done, and he promises me I can help with the music department's next CD cover. That night, I'm so excited at the prospect of doing something artistic at work that I can't sleep. Day 126: My boss asks me to fax over the specs for the next CD cover to the artist they always use. He refuses to meet my eyes. Later that day, I notice that my coworker is wearing jeans. I realize that she often wears jeans. No one's said a word.

MICKEY Z.: For six years I worked as a trainer and gym floor manager at the Vertical Club. What Studio 54 was to 1970s New York, the Vertical Club (VC) was to 1980s New York. A warehouse-sized health club, complete with neon lights and blaring dance music, it was where the Big Apple's social elite came to sweat, strain, moan, groan, and gyrate—occasionally, they even worked out (sorry, I couldn't resist). The job paid like shit and many of the rich clientele treated us like peons, but I made some great friends and felt a genuine camaraderie with my fellow workers. Overall, the place was a high-end lunatic asylum. One episode captures that job and that time period best. The many labyrinthine stairways at the Vertical Club served many purposes—a "lounge" area for the underpaid trainers or a secret hideaway for sex, doing drugs, etc. These hideaways also provided a comfortable home for a female Verticalite who was reduced to offering sexual favors to the porters in order to have a roof over her head. The presence of Paula in the bowels of the gym was a well-kept secret among a select few for some time. The VC's upper echelon of management chose to ignore her presence and the many Spanish-speaking porters who frequented all areas of the facility spoke of her in hushed and knowing tones. That is, until a coat belonging to an aerobics teacher disappeared one night. She asked for help and the staff searched the gym fruitlessly before bringing the matter to the attention of the health club's vice president. This VC mainstay was notorious for having the demeanor of an attack dog and changing moods at the drop of a Nautilus pin. Needless to say, the aerobics teacher was dismissed after being the target of an inarticulate tirade about leaving her property unguarded. The matter seemed to be over until the next day when myself and another gym employee were give ourselves a guided tour of the notorious rendezvous spots in the massive spa. Upon opening a well-hidden door that leads to a catwalk above the gym, I was stunned to find a woman sleeping under a blanket. I closed the door and asked my tour partner about this. He happened to be Spanish and he told me of rumors from the porters about "Paula" who lived in the gym and would have sex with them. We headed back to the gym floor to decide what to do about Paula when we suddenly noticed that she had followed us out into the club. I immediately recognized the coat she was wearing as belonging to the aerobics teachers. We had found our thief. Like Starsky and Hutch, we followed Paula onto the elevator and proceeded to question her about the coat. Instinctively, she went on the offensive and grew indignant that anyone would accuse her of such a thing. As this situation became more and more amusing, I backed off and watched as she bought an orange drink from the juice bar and calmly exited the gym. All this was reported to the bosses and was greeted with knowing nods and grins. The story I got was that Paula was a member of the gym who had hit the skids. She lost her job and got evicted from her apartment, so she used her expired Vertical Club membership card to sneak in. To this day, I don't know whatever happened to her.

SANDER HICKS: I used to sing this song, about Kinko's:

"Marty, this is the best job I've ever had.
But that's not saying much. Kinko's is kind of bad."

MAKING YOUR MOVE

(TRANSITIONS)

MANNY SIVERIO: Then I got into the stunt business. My close friend and partner, Jeff Ward, was working as a stunt man on a feature called *Spike of Bensonhurst*. He knew the stunt coordinator, Jery Hewitt, was looking for several Hispanics for a fight scene and that was the beginning of what has become a career for me.

A.D. NAUMAN: The pressure started to increase. I finished my Master's program in education, and started to dream of bigger and better things: a Ph.D. With a Ph.D., I could be a college professor, I thought, and be safe forever from the business world, safe from cubicles and temp agencies and secretaries who hated me. I started the Ph.D. program, which was about a thousand times more difficult than the Master's. Also, my agent was unable to sell my two novels and had reached the point of giving up. I suffered a lot over that; there were long nights of angry thoughts and tears and finally prayers. Also, I was thirty and beginning to worry about having children. The best years were coming to an end.

INDIO: I started to get heavy with the drugs, lost my apartment, became homeless, started sellin' *Street News* in December1989. I got busted, went upstate for 6 months 'n went to live with my daughter in Queens. I went back to sellin' papers at *Crossroads* magazine, a homeless newspaper in 1990 'n went back to *Street News* around 1991. I have been there ever since 'n became the editor 'n chief in 1996. I do not get a salary 'n I do it for free.

RACHEL F.: One of my freelance jobs was especially interesting, and involved a great deal of stimulating detective work and correspondence with associates in many countries. This job had an especially pleasant physical environment— relaxed and sunny, in a casual downtown neighborhood; we played music. There were no cubicles, nor were our desks in little rows. I worked with pleasant people, and I was bestowed with important responsibilities. I made exciting business trips to three foreign countries for my company. I decided to cut back my other jobs, and work most of my time at this one. They had asked me to work as many hours as I could, still leaving the "when" and "how many" up to me.

TIM WISE: In 1995 I started going out on the lecture circuit, having gotten picked up by a radical agency in California: Speak Out. I got to do that because of the anti-Duke work I had done, and because I marketed myself well to them: as young white southerner who would go in and kick some white folks in the ass about racism. And they liked the idea, so they added me to the bureau. Pretty soon, the demand was through the roof. Lots of schools wanted a white guy to talk about these things because they knew that their mostly white students would never listen to the same radical message from a person of color. The rest is history. I've been doing it ever since.

RICHARD MILLER: I now drive an ice cream truck. The gig actually came to me from a customer at Broadway Natural. He offered me the gig and after a few months we started talking about varied topics, and found a strange sort of parallel in a lot of our values; no, he's not vegan, but he has a heightened awareness of the absurdity of our world. I took the job and was promptly fired from the health food store. My route is on the Lower East Side, so there are quite a few vegan choices along the way. The truck has a generator, multiple outlets, and running water, which is ideal for the juicing I will be doing during my long summer shifts. As strange as this sounds this job offers me the most freedom I've had in my employment history; no time clock, no office, virtually constant motion, no two days the same, no paperwork...the list of perks is long.

SETH ASHER: Some other stations along the way from financial advisor to massage therapist: substitute teacher in NYC public school system and Transportation Alternatives staff member. These "experiments" were greatly enlightening, as they were also, at times, frustrating. The TA job really socked me in the stomach, as I naively thought that it would be the dream job for this staunch believer in the virtue of non-automobile transportation. The reasons for this disappointing turn of events are complex. But certainly one factor was that I expected this job to finally be, after so much emotional defeat toiling in a society that seemed all wrong, *the* long-awaited big solution. Naturally when I felt inadequately supported and even treated with hostility from a co-worker, occurrences that can happen even in a good work situation, I was way too emotionally charged to deal effectively with the situation. The public school teaching environment was extremely dysfunctional. This made me appreciate the frustration of striving to rise above trying circumstances. Knowing that one is doing potentially honorable and meaningful worker is, by itself, not enough. Pleasant working conditions, being treated respectfully and being appreciated are as important as anything else about a job, regardless of how noble the cause might be.

JASON KUCSMA: One of the most interesting jobs I have had involved being a phone tester for a civil rights law firm. The law firm was on the west coast and had been commissioned to test an insurance company for racial bias as part of an out-of-court settlement made by a national insurance company. We were responsible for testing the corporation's offices in Northwest Ohio. The insurance company had been accused of racial bias in how they provide quotes for homeowner's insurance, and it was our job to test the company to make sure they were making good on the settlement to agree to terminate such practices. I did this for two summers for a couple months each summer. I was the control of the test, so each week I would get a profile of a house and call an agent to get a quote for the house I was buying. After I reported my findings to my coordinator, an African American male would call the same agent about a similar house in a different neighborhood, usually a predominately working class or "undesirable" neighborhood. The job was pretty fascinating and I enjoyed the covertness of the whole project. Since I had to sign a confidentiality agreement, there was cloak of mystery around this summer job and I wasn't allowed to tell anyone about the work I was doing.

MICKEY Z.: I worked at a video store during the early days of the VCR (got fired). I cleaned cars at a car rental place (fired again). For years, I proofread bad books for a vanity press (yep, fired). I sang in a rock band that never gigged and I managed a heavy metal that played many gigs. I've trained clients, taught martial arts, given seminars on vegetarianism and writing. The best job I ever had was editor of *Curio Magazine*. If *Curio* didn't fold, that's where I'd be right now. As of this writing, I just started working on a newspaper called *Wide Angle*.

RACHEL F.: I remember the new anxiety of having a job that I truly cared about. When I had worked at various jobs, it had been a great source of security to know that I did not depend on any one of them. Now I placed most of my "eggs in one basket." I enjoyed the small theatre-related company much more than any of my other jobs, and felt myself an integral, important part of its management. I had to admit to myself that I would hate to lose this job. This was an entirely new feeling. I have to say "most of my eggs" rather than "all," because I still take the occasional side job doing gardening, bookkeeping, office or home organizing, and also sales for a friend. I help small businesses set themselves up on book-keeping software and teach them its use. Knowing these options are still there provides a certain reassurance, but I now depend on my main job for 90 percent of my income.

MICKEY Z.: I was once the managing editor of a third-rate porno magazine but I made sure to sneak in radical propaganda throughout the mag and some Situationist rants into the girl copy. I worked in a cubicle and had to wear a tie for that gig, but took solace in, say, making a major porn star spout off about the misery of everyday life in a society of the spectacle.

CHRISTINE HAMM: On Day 143, along with twenty percent of the staff, I am laid off because the church has mishandled funds. We are given two hours notice. After I was gone, my boss sat on the step of the building and smoked and cried, telling anyone who would listen that he had just lost the best secretary of his life. Someone who worked for a different corporation in that same building listened so on Day 144 I am hired to work for the CEO...of the Lutheran Church. This story inspired a poem:

THE BAD SECRETARY

She weeps into your coffee; staples memos to her blouse. She has acne; her lipstick smears. She breaks up with her boyfriend every other weekend and makes you hear about it. She is always twenty minutes late. She sometimes answers the phone with a stunned silence, as if she's forgotten not only where she works and who she is, but what a phone is. She loses files. She erases files. She gets a manicure once a week and has sunsets painted on her nails. Her nails are so long she can't type. She has carpal tunnel so she can't type. She shows up one Monday in a neck brace. She forgets to wear a bra. She swears (a lot). She refuses to get you lunch. You find a voodoo doll of yourself in her desk. She makes you hate her. She smells of cinnamon and dog shit. When she wears a tank top, you swear you see the flutter of wings around her shoulder blades. Your palm pilot melts in its cradle. Your tie makes like a lobster and pinches your nose. Your titanium G-4 explodes. You can't stop yourself from putting your tongue in her mouth. She doesn't wear underwear. She doesn't bathe. She makes you love her. She is your master.

RUSS KICK: Working for the Man sucks overall, but it does teach you an awful lot about people.

Lack of money is the root of all evil.
—BERNARD SHAW

THE DARK SIDE

(ILLEGAL JOBS)

RACHEL MORIELLO: My most lucrative job was when I earned $200 bucks to watch these people have sex at the W Hotel off of Union Square. I didn't have to do anything but watch and I was only there for about half-hour. It was definitely weird but it was pretty easy money. I knew the people so I wasn't scared for my well being or anything. Is that illegal? No, right?

MANNY SIVERIO: I have to say that I'm fearful of the law and respect it, so to my knowledge I can't say I've ever done an illegal job.

SANDER HICKS: No comment.

SUSANA SANTIZO: I hustled my last year in high school. I was tired of holding down a job and going to school. I never got to be a kid, so I figured, go to school and sell the nicks I got from Harlem to the rich kids for dimes. I stopped once I graduated and started again once I moved out on my own. I quit my job when my supervisor told me it wasn't appropriate to tell a child "I LOVE YOU" because I was just a nanny. So I told her to go fuck herself and went back to slinging. I made $1400 in 3 days. I made rent, my bills and started to save for my book.

SPARROW: I guess I'm not a very illegal person; I can't think of criminal jobs I have taken. At Cornell University, when I banged my knee sliding down a snow slope on a cafeteria tray, the clinic gave me Darvon. I didn't like the pill—too soporific—so I hustled the drug at the Noyes Student Center. "Darvon, Darvon!" I muttered. Finally, a young brown-haired guy was curious. But I didn't charge him. I just gave him the bright orange pills. I dislike profit.

MICKEY Z.: I sold pot when I was 14 (until my sister's boyfriend kicked my ass for it). Then there was the five-finger discount at Gimbel's and the job where I was somehow made responsible for doing payroll (let's leave it at that).

TIM WISE: Before the Patriot Act, I would say none of my jobs were illegal. Now it's an open question I guess as to whether anything I do is still legal.

Work is a four-letter word.
—THE SMITHS (MORRISSEY)

SOULS FOR SALE

(SELLING OUT, GOING MAINSTREAM,
WEARING A TIE)

GREG RAPAPORT: I'd rather put my head in a wood chipper than work in a cubicle and no suit currently resides in my closet.

RUSS KICK: I've never had a button-down job. Haven't been a cubicle monkey. I've worn a nametag at most of my retail jobs (which have been all of my jobs except for construction). It was always creepy to have a complete stranger call me by my name. I wore steel-toed work boots during my week of literal ditch digging.

RACHEL MORIELLO: The biggest sell-out job was either the one driving the scab van that I mentioned earlier or promoting products on the street that I would never use, like cold medicines. I had a lot of "near-brushes" with sell-out jobs that I was never able to bring myself to do. For example, I trained to do promotions for Marlboro cigarettes but I left halfway through—I couldn't do it! I also almost went to a Christmas party for some bigwig jerk-off where they were going to pay me just to wear a short dress and "mingle," but I couldn't bring myself to do that either.

CHAZ MENA: I don't think that I have ever had a 9-5, mainstream job. Even teaching in Miami was a master class where I was tied up only 12-15 hours a week. Everything else that I have earned has been through my acting or my itinerant jobs. Examples include:
  -Translator/Interpreter
  -Mailroom in publishing
  -Copy editor in advertising
  -Freelance account executive in advertising
  -Substitute teaching
  -Stage carpenter
  -Security at MTV Music Awards
  -Bookseller, retail
  -Research librarian
  -Waiter

GEORGIA GIANNIKOURIS: One summer when I was fifteen I decided to take a job offer from my aunt in an insurance firm. That's when I made my decision that I'd never be able to work a nine to five cubicle job. I'm still firm on that.

GARY BADDELEY: Richard [Metzger, co-founder of The Disinformation Company] and I have always said that we'd sell out if we got the chance! Last year one of our gang posted a fake press release on April Fools Day saying that our company had been acquired by AOL Time Warner. You'd be amazed how many people believed it. We wish it were true. What we really mean is that we'd like to have dollops of OPM to do more of what we're doing now.

INDIO: Yes, I think about goin' mainstream. When I am low on funds 'n I get into that self-pity bag.

MICKEY Z.: I've done work that could easily be deemed "mainstream" by some. Hey, I'm working at a corporate gym right now and I even have a book coming out that is not exactly radical. As for *really* going mainstream, I'd choose it over homelessness.

RACHEL MORIELLO: I could never work in an office. Sometimes I think about becoming a full-time teacher for the benefits and security, but I always end up thinking differently.

A.D. NAUMAN: I am sitting here this very moment tempted to go mainstream. I guess I had unrealistic expectations about what would happen after publishing my first novel. In fact, there were absolutely no tickertape parades, and I did not ascend to heaven. In fact, nothing much happened at all. I think that, to get noticed, books need a big push from a big publisher. And what's going to get you that? A book that is easily categorizable, Oprah book clubbish, with a distinct market. Something original—truly literary—seems to confuse agents and editors today. (This is partly what *Scorch* is about: how the marketplace acts as a censor on originality.) If you have a well-known author backing you, telling the publishers to publish your book, then they'll do it. (Unfortunately, I don't have that.) So I'm sitting here discouraged and wondering if I should try to write something more conventional. I don't delude myself thinking that would be easy: it would take a great deal of time, energy, and talent. And then in the end you would have written...an ordinary book. You would have strived toward and achieved the ordinary. (Still, I haven't ruled it out.) I guess what we eventually face is that remaining true to our own vision (and working hard) will not necessarily translate to popular success. That is especially true today. Publishing companies are not really interested in publishing books; they're interested in making profits. So they pursue celebrities: celebrity authors and celebrity Congressional interns. The whole situation is quite awful. My dream for my own work is not that it will get me big bucks. I have to wonder about people who think they're going to make a lot of money writing. A few people do, but if money is what you're after, you should put your energies into sales or banking or some industry that's more reliable. My dream for my work is that it will be read, by as many people as possible, and cause people to think.

JASON KUCSMA: This was my intention with my stint at the university. I thought I could do fairly liberal/mainstream teaching work while doing my other projects on the side. However, I abandoned this notion as I realized how time-consuming teaching/academia was for me and how stressful I found the work to be. Last semester, I taught a class part-time as a favor to the ACS program. I thought I was getting a good deal because I would be teaching three times a week and making about $1900 over the semester. After all the time I spent grading and doing lesson plans (not to mention the undocumented time I spent worrying or thinking about my class), I was making less than $6 an hour.

PAMELA RICE: I could go mainstream at any time, I suppose. I would do it under dire financial circumstances—more dire than I'm living under now.

SANDER HICKS: My mind has the capacity to imagine a lot of different scenarios; it also has the capacity to fool itself into thinking I would be happy in a place that has proven to be bad for me. I'd rather work construction to stay afloat. The money's not bad, and I like the camaraderie. Yes, I got fired last week, but I was back to work a day later. This guy on my crew intervened with the psycho boss.

GREG RAPAPORT: I've considered going mainstream and then I came to my senses and realized that I'm not built for it.

RACHEL F.: Working in the law firm's corporate-oriented environment, I experienced for the first time a sense of suffocation, so to speak. I had a sense of having to play a certain part, as in a theatrical role, to maintain the illusion of the personae required for the department. I was conscious that I needed to stifle various aspects of my personality in order to fill the role—that who I naturally was would be considered inappropriate. It's not that I was particularly outrageous. I was well mannered, well-spoken, from a middle class background. Maybe I felt myself to be much more expressive and open than would have been appropriate. Maybe the atmosphere represented the suburbs I had grown up in and fled from. Certainly there was a uniform. I had to have an entire wardrobe of business clothes that did not express who I was at all, and in fact hid it. At least that is how I felt at that age and time.

GEORGIA GIANNIKOURIS: When I was in high school I went through a time of serious depression. I was at such a low that I felt lost every day of my life. I wrote furiously and feverously during that time. In the little world I was trapped in, I had millions of bursting emotions that wanted to bust out of my body in colored pieces of confetti. And I wrote it all down—my heart always pumping and hand pressed against the paper. I HATED the word "normal." When I read that writing now, I know that from as far back as I can remember, I have hated normality and MAINSTREAM. It's horrid. And boring. And completely uninteresting. A lot is going on inside me, and I'm prepared to act on it with every ounce of energy I possess.

JEN ANGEL: Yep, I'm working in a regular job now, trying to keep other projects afloat. I work at Planned Parenthood. It's like working for a doctor's office, except that it's a non-profit organization which is cool, and also we really serve a population that needs the services. It's good, but it's also stressful because like most non-profits, there's never any money and all that.

RUSS KICK: Since my realization at age 30, I've never been tempted to go back to mainstream work.

CHRISTINA MOSES: I have considered doing mainstream jobs.... I don't mean restaurants...that's pretty mainstream ... and that's where most of my "work experience" lies. I mean corporate office jobs. I CAN'T AND WILL NOT. I don't do well as a secretary or administrative assistant. It doesn't work for me. The only thing that I am going to do that is mainstream is working as a production assistant for commercials and feature films. I learn so much that way about what it takes to make a film and to produce. I don't believe that it is the only way to become a director. I don't think I have to slave away years and years and climb up the totem pole. I definitely don't want to rely on that. It is experience. It provides tools to take with me for when I begin to make my own documentaries. And, the money really helps. It's not a whole of money, but it is consistent. I get to exercise my brain as opposed to earning inconsistent money serving food or seating folks down to eat. I don't devalue restaurant or night club work. It's just not for me anymore.

RACHEL F.: I think there's a danger in assuming that the person in the mainstream is a slave, and the person on the "alternative" track is independent. For example, an artist could be obsessed with – ruled by – the opinions of the circles he or she travels in, no matter how out in the margin.

JASON KUCSMA: I suppose the closest I will come to doing more mainstream, full-time work will be teaching at a community college or university. I haven't thought much about how or when I plan to cash in on my master's degree, but I know it's there if I need it. My real plan "B" is to go back to school to get my degree in Library Science. I worked one semester as a graduate advisor in the Music Library and Sound Recording Archives at the university and I really loved the environment. I liked being able to help people find resources and information for the work they were doing.

SUSANA SANTIZO: I'll work anywhere but an office. I make money to do all the things I want and need to do. It's just a fact of my life.

GEORGIA GIANNIKOURIS: School can actually be an attempt to go mainstream. Choosing a major is like choosing a life sentence and everyone has something to say about it. It is a constant whirl of heart vs. head, heart vs. mom and dad, heart vs. practical. I am both impractical and illogical to a certain extent, so the battle gets confusing. I've fluctuated between art history, independent major (something I make up which would include everything I adore), fine arts, psychology, urban studies, and the thought of business crossed my mind for a split second, but the cringing motion I did lasted much longer. We pay all this money, too, so we want to be sure our major is something that we could put to use. So, it's like, "Well I *wanna* take artsy classes and sociology classes and English classes, but then what do I do with that? Maybe I should take a major like finance. Cringe. Yeah right." Finally I selected to double major in Sociology and Communications and to complete a certificate program in Peace and Justice Studies. Hooray for me! Ask me what I'm planning on doing with this, and I get fidgety. If you're someone who is interesting and who is inspiring, and who I think is a believer of dreams, I will sit and explain. If you're not, then most likely I'll tell you I don't know yet. But it ain't easy having people around you (who really care about you), telling you they want the best for you and would love it if you chose a more "secure" path to follow. Ahem. I'm 21 now. I am aware how responsible I am for my own decisions. ;-)

SPARROW: Suddenly, at the age of 48, I realize what I'd like to be: Secretary of State! I find myself thinking of John Milton (the poet) who was Latin secretary for Cromwell, and Geoffrey Chaucer (the poet), who was comptroller of customs on wool and hides at London (1374-86).

In America, it's not black and white justice, it's green justice. In America, you're innocent till proven broke."
—WILL DURST

THIS IS NOT AN EXIT

(FIRED, DOWNSIZED, QUIT)

GARY BADDELEY: I've quit a couple of times, but only in the context of moving to another job, never in disgust. I've never been fired, although when Razorfish Studios was going down the tubes and I was "negotiating" to reacquire The Disinformation Company, I'm sure that I would have been fired had I not been very, very careful to make sure that I didn't do anything that would have given rise to a fireable offense.

JEN ANGEL: I've quit a whole bunch of times. I've been fired twice. When I worked at a recycling center at the Ohio State campus, we would drive around to the different buildings and pick up the paper and soda cans. One morning at like 7 PM, I was in the truck with this other guy driving, and he hit a parked car when he was trying to back up to a loading dock. Everyone in the truck got fired. Of course it was lame because I hadn't done anything, but obviously it was everyone's responsibility, right?

PAMELA RICE: Fired twice, restructured once. Quit many. So far, I can count being fired as the worst thing to ever happen to me. I was told that I can call myself lucky if this is really the case.

JASON KUCSMA: I've never been fired or downsized. I did quit a job at the UPS hub here in Toledo. I worked there for three weeks. They have this job where you can be a "sorter" on the lines. It's more desirable than loading or unloading the trucks. Basically you have to sort the packages as they come down the line to make sure they go to the right trucks. In order to qualify for this job, you had to sit through two to three weeks of class where you memorized zip codes and corresponding conveyor belt colors. So I sat through this class for two and half weeks, dragging my feet through the whole process so I wouldn't have to go out to the line a minute before I had to. They had tests that we had to pass before we could go out on the line and I purposely failed tests so I could stay in the class as long as possible. When I couldn't stall any longer, I passed my last test and went out on the line. I stayed there for about one week and then quit. It was ridiculous. They bragged about how you only had to work about four hours a day, but they squeezed a full-day's work into half as much time.

SUSANA SANTIZO: I have never been fired. If I do something I always put a hundred percent into it. I quit every single job I had ever had—that's about 10. The longest I've ever held a job was 3 years, my present job.

MANNY SIVERIO: During my tenure at the health club I was "laid off." Those were the words they used. Since then I've technically been working for myself.

GREG RAPAPORT: I never got fired. I quit all my jobs because they were dead end jobs and didn't allow any creativity or growth.

JEN ANGEL: Last year I got fired from this distribution company I worked at. I was really shocked that the owner fired me. He's like my age, and though he can be well intentioned at times, he didn't know how to be a manager or how to communicate with his employees. There were like 8 or 10 employees, including his wife and her sister. I worked there about a year and a half and we all worked pretty independently of each other. I enjoyed it for the most part, but it was really stressful. There was a lot of tension between me and the owner over various things, and neither of us communicated very well with the other. It had gotten to the point where I would do things without caring whether or not he would care. I would tell him straight up I thought he was lame, I would be mad and stressed out all the time. I threatened to quit a couple of times. I thought he would never have the guts to do it, because he had tried to fire this other guy a few months before and the guy had lingered on for weeks. In retrospect, I should have left sooner, because I was really stressed out all the time and taking it out on the people around me, and it was just a bad situation. Things are much better since then, so it worked out great, though he's continued to be a jerk to me since then. Thank goodness I don't see him around town or anything.

MARTA RUSSELL: I was fired once. My career in the commercial film business ended due to being fired when my impairment progressed and my then-employer perceived me as a liability and got rid of me—in a New York second. I was on the job one day and then told not to come back, no reason given. In America an employer can fire anyone at anytime. This was prior to the Americans with Disabilities Act which may or may not have helped in my case to provide me with a "reasonable accommodation" given that employers prevail in 93 percent of the employment discrimination cases brought to court and 80 percent of employees cases are thrown out on summary judgment. Anyway, I was treated like dirt.

SANDER HICKS: I've been fired probably about 5 times.

RACHEL MORIELLO: I usually quit when I can't take it anymore... I have only been fired twice: Once from a restaurant job. They called me and fired me over the phone on Valentine's Day, which was fine because I hated that job. The other was from my first professional acting job. I was doing a play aboard this boat in New Hampshire. I was a college senior and I thought I was hot because I had gone out and got myself a "real" acting job (when I wasn't cast in the theatre department's main stage production). It was the day after Thanksgiving and I had to drive all the way from New Paltz, NY to Portsmith, NH for a show that night. When I got into town I was about two hours early. I was really tired so I decided to take a nap and I over-slept and missed the boat. That definitely humbled me, and I've never done that again.

HAVE YOU EVER RECEIVED UNEMPLOYMENT INSURANCE OR WORKER'S COMP?

GARY BADDELEY: Yes. Don't tell my dad.

PAMELA RICE: I've collected unemployment about 3 times, I believe. I'm very grateful that it was there for me.

SANDER HICKS: Hah ha, no. I once slashed my thumb with a box cutter at the 1991 drugstore job. I even passed out; it was gruesome. I filed for Worker's Comp but I never got anything, not even a straight answer. Ah, Virginia.

JEN ANGEL: Yeah, after that guy fired me from the distribution company, I got unemployment for about 2 months. It was great. It was about half what I had been making, but I probably could have lived on that for a while. So even though I should have left that job sooner, I wouldn't have been able to get unemployment if he hadn't fired me, so that was a stroke of luck.

MARTA RUSSELL: I went on SSDI, public disability insurance. Even though I have cerebral palsy, it was first denied to me and I had a lengthy arduous fight to get it. This is when I realized that the social safety net wasn't so "safe."

RACHEL MORIELLO: I was on unemployment in 2001 for about 8 months.

MICKEY Z.: After being fired from the porno mag, I had to go to court and fight for my benefits, but I won (thanks to a lawyer friend, Darnay Hoffman). Unemployment insurance is the closest thing this country has to genuine subsidized arts.

No one should ever work. Work is the source of nearly all the misery in the world. Almost any evil you'd care to name comes from working or from living in a world designed for work. In order to stop suffering, we have to stop working.
—BOB BLACK

WAGE AGAINST THE MACHINE

(FINANCIAL STATEMENTS)

HOW WOULD DESCRIBE YOUR CURRENT FINANCIAL SITUATION?

PAMELA RICE: Precarious. I am entirely dependent on my husband who is a day trader.

SANDER HICKS: A challenge.

SPARROW: Apparently, the finances of my household are a success, at the moment. (My wife actually totals up all the bills and the money in our accounts.) My wife enjoys working, and is making a lot of money—or a lot of money for the Catskills, where we live, in an apartment. Violet is a reporter for *The Phoenicia Times*, *The Woodstock Times*; also a photographer for *The Phoenicia Times*. She teaches nature-lore to a group of young teenagers on Fridays. Also, she works at the Phoenicia Library (at this very moment, in fact). I write for *The Phoenicia Times* (as a gossip columnist) and for *Chronogram*, an arts journal of the Hudson Valley (a personal-journal column). Sometimes *The Sun*, a magazine in North Carolina, publishes my essays. Our parents give us money on holidays (my in-laws gave us a thousand dollars for Christmas, my parents sent $500 for Hanukkah). Also I am a substitute teacher, a couple days a week.

GARY BADDELEY: My financial situation is in some ways better and in some ways worse than it was five years ago. Back then I was making some pretty good money in the record business. Now I'm lucky if I can pay myself at all. On the other hand, I do have various investments and the last five years has been a good time to be an investor, unless you parked all your money in Enron or Razorfish, or their ilk. I also married a scientist/doctor who makes some decent money herself.

MARTA RUSSELL: I live on below poverty level disability benefits which I supplement by selling articles and commentaries. I have an attendant who helps me with tasks in my home. One must stay destitute to keep these services though disability activists have been working hard to change the rules so one can work without losing one's public health care or attendant. I don't expect any big change in my financial predicament in the future.

GEORGIA GIANNIKOURIS: Right now I am in my third year of college—just beginning my own road. It is safe to say that my financial situation isn't exactly a good one. Anybody who is in college at this point can agree. I've always been extremely independent, and I am adamant about making my own money. I've been working for a long time, and I don't mind it at all, but it has been impossible to save any of it when school tuition and general daily expenses leave your pockets empty.

GREG RAPAPORT: My current financial situation is good but could be better. My wife has a great job so between her and me and my business we manage to live somewhat comfortably.

CHRISTINE HAMM: I've accepted that I'm never going to be rich and that I'm always going to be struggling financially, which means I'll probably never have a car or house or maybe even children. I've sort of defined myself as living on the margins of society. Of course, society has many margins, and mine is the artistic one. It's difficult to find people that live in and believe in the same subculture, but New York City is one of the best, and most infamous, places.

MANNY SIVERIO: I would say that overall my financial situation has greatly improved over the last 10 years once I found my niche in the film business and learned how to channel my skills into it. It's a matter of learning how to play the game. But first I had to learn the rules. Once I learned the rules, it was a matter of changing them around and playing them so that it could work for me.

MICKEY Z.: My financial situation is perpetually in flux. I've finally conceded the need to spend less time writing and more time earning money so that has resulted in increased income. However, my chosen field of earning (personal fitness training) is unpredictable. I'm extremely fortunate that my wife earns a steady income doing something she (usually) likes and she is (almost always) supportive of my quixotic efforts.

JEN ANGEL: Well, I make $10.40 an hour and I work full time. Between rent, student loans, living expenses, and the massive debt I've built up from working on media projects, I pretty much live paycheck to paycheck. It helps that I live very simply and don't spend a lot of money on stuff like clothes or records—though I do have a lot of books. Also, I live in an area that is very cheap (we have a nice 3 bedroom apartment with garage and basement, central air, etc. for $600 a month plus utilities), and that allows me to spend more money on projects, or rather, on paying down debt, than living elsewhere would. Also, I'm not married with two kids or a mortgage—I think living simply and "non-traditionally" in a lot of ways, I'm able to get by with less. I've also had pretty good luck and haven't had to deal with major car repairs or accidents or health care costs.

SETH ASHER: I'm secure and happy in this area. I've never felt more confident in my ability to manage resources. I have some savings, which helps. Also reassuring is the knowledge that as a massage therapist I have the ability to earn a living while providing what is, in my opinion, an unquestionably valuable and healthful service. But my contentment in this area has been attained only through a changed worldview. In my former yuppie days, which were flush with cash, money was much more of a concern and source of stress. This was relieved only after coming to genuinely understand that health and happiness can not be purchased. On the contrary, a money-centered existence tends to degrade the individual. And money-centeredness usually goes hand in hand with degradation of our planet and its inhabitants. My spending level has greatly dropped in the last four and a half years in tandem with attaining self-reliance, resourceful collaboration and responsibility, all of which have been profoundly empowering for me.

CHRISTINA MOSES: My current financial situation? Well...hmmmm...isn't so hot at the moment. I am in debt with school loans and credit cards I used in college. I have not saved so I am living hand to mouth at the moment. This is the lowest my financial situation has ever been. My choice to earn a living as an artist at the moment is hard on my finances. Acting is a hard field to break into and to actually earn a living at it. Especially the area that inspires and fuels me, which is theatre. Photography is highly competitive and if you are not into fashion, money is not usually abundant right off the bat. What I have chosen to pursue doesn't in and of itself a huge money maker, but I have to follow my heart, and I know that I am always taken care of and always will be.

TIM WISE: My current situation is quite good. Very comfortable. Certainly making more money than I would have expected for doing radical political work.

SUSANA SANTIZO: I am currently at my lowest point. I was making more money 4 years ago when I was a receptionist in a chiropractor's office. I'm much happier now, but I'm a realist and I know that happiness don't pay the bills so I have to find a job that will. I use to bartend and I plan on going back real soon so I could write during the day and work at night.

RUSS KICK: Pathetic. As I write this, I'm dodging calls from my credit card bank. It seems that they expect me to pay them. The grocery store where my ladylove and I do our shopping won't accept my checks anymore. This might be the biggest lesson of all to those who give up the workaday world: don't expect to live well. You'll probably bounce some checks, be medically uninsured, and not be able to afford anything but the necessities, for a while anyway. No doubt there are a few people who jump right in and make a good living, but expect to live frugally for at least a few years.

RACHEL MORIELLO: I am staying afloat! I just about break-even every month; never any extra money but I can pay my bills.

JASON KUCSMA: I currently volunteer a majority of my waking hours for *Clamor* magazine and I also work part time at a locally owned copy/print shop (about 25-30 hours a week). I live on about $250 a week and try to ignore the student loan debts that seem like they will be forever in deferment.

A.D. NAUMAN: Amazingly, right now I'm doing okay monetarily. I'm almost out of debt, which had been substantial. I expect the future to be even brighter. This financial upturn is, of course, completely unrelated to my artistic endeavors. In 1994, when I received the Illinois Arts Council Award, I took the $1000 award money and opened a special bank account for "all my writing money," which I was then going to use for traveling to Europe. After several years, that account got up to, oh, about $1050. Eventually I had to use it for rent.

CONTRAST THAT WITH, SAY, FIVE YEARS AGO.

PAMELA RICE: Precarious. I was working, mostly freelance, as a computer graphics person, while spending huge amounts of time trying to build a vegetarian advocacy organization.

SANDER HICKS: These days, it's less money, but a better life. About five years ago, I was still occasionally working at Kinko's. Work there was interesting occasionally, but most of the time degrading, you really felt like no one cared, even though on the surface the company was what I call "hippie capitalist." The employees were called "coworkers" and there was a "progressive" statement of principles on the wall. As if to say, there's something wrong with capitalism, we know that, we will attempt to hide the stink, but we cannot remove the shit.

CHRISTINA MOSES: Five years ago I was still in college, but I was living in Santa Cruz, California. I received a huge scholarship from the school, and I was working in a group home for autistic children which paid very well. Plus the cost of living in Cali is A LOT less than the Big Apple.

SPARROW: Five years ago, financial life was easier for us. We lived in the East Village (Manhattan); I worked 15 hours a week at the 92nd Street Y; my wife was a part-time computer programmer. I made $25 an hour; Violet made $50 per hour. Due to our friend who sublet us our apartment, we paid only $400 a month rental.

JEN ANGEL: Things are pretty much the same as they were five years ago. This is the most I have ever made on a consistent basis, though I've only had this job for six months, and have never had one job more than a year and a half. When I lived in San Francisco, I would temp for $15 an hour, but the work was very inconsistent and I could go two weeks without an assignment, so that doesn't really count.

TIM WISE: Five years ago, I was just beginning to build a reputation on the lecture circuit and among my peers in the antiracism community. I was taking lots of speaking gigs and research contracts for very low pay, just to be doing the work, and to improve my skills, my knowledge base, etc. Even now I don't charge an outrageous amount, but I am more in control of that than I was then, at which time I pretty much had to take anything that came my way. And five years ago, in turn was far better than the five prior to that, during which time I was truly struggling to be taken seriously as well as to be paid.

JASON KUCSMA: Five years ago, I thought I would probably finish my graduate work (with a PhD) and work as a professor teaching cultural studies and publishing valuable research on the left. I've since abandoned this idea when I became disenchanted with the amount of bureaucracy in academic institutions and the lack of connection I saw between academia and real world issues. I guess I had thought that the academy was going to be a place where I could do pretty important radical work, but I just don't see it as that place anymore. The more I got involved in school and my studies, the more I realized that the people I admired for doing real, grassroots political work were rarely doing it in conjunction with academic institutions.

RACHEL MORIELLO: Five years ago, and even much more recently, I have been dirt broke. I mean not a cent to my name. I have been there so many times; it is very scary. When I first came to the city, I used credit cards all the time, even for groceries, because I had nothing. Eventually all the cards got maxed out and I started to sink into major debt. Now I use no credit cards, I am completely opposed to them, and encourage everyone I know to be completely free of their innocuous form of SLAVERY. In 2001, I was finally able to settle all of my credit cards, wiping out over $17,000 in debt. I will never go back.

WHAT ARE YOUR FINANCIAL EXPECTATIONS IN THIS AREA OVER THE NEXT FEW YEARS?

GREG RAPAPORT: I'm hoping to establish myself as a semi-professional musician meaning that I make a fairly substantial second income from CD sales. I also hope to retain some additional institutional clients for my business.

PAMELA RICE: A lot depends upon donors to the non-profit (VivaVegie Society) that I set up. Our funding comes in small amounts from individual donors. Our veggie politics are too radical for the major institutional givers. So far there is little precedent for groups like ours to get big grants. Most donations come in amounts of $50 or less. Unfortunately, perhaps, the group's success may come by default, that is, at the expense of the meat industry itself. So many disasters have meat consumption as their root cause. And the disasters abound: Mad cow disease and hoof-and-mouth disease, bacterial contamination and antibiotic resistance, global fish extinction, nitrogen and phosphorous runoff from factory farms, desertification from overgrazing, awareness of animal cruelty in today's animal agriculture, as well as the many health epidemics caused by meat (heart failure, diabetes, and obesity to name just a few). A mad cow disease outbreak, alone, could have people running to our veggie center. Sudden support could get us that prized storefront—something we have been hoping for years. We could be poised to be great beneficiaries during times of colossal troubles experienced by our opposition. This, however, is not the scenario I hope for.

SANDER HICKS: Well I'm out here on Long Island trying to write and sell a book about Karl Rove.

JEN ANGEL: I also feel that I'm getting older and to the point where I'm going to become less and less employable at a "real" job. This year, for example, I worked for four different companies. I've never had a job for over two years at a time, and because I lack any kind of specialized skills, I'm pretty over-qualified for a lot of jobs. I mean, I know a little about a lot of things, but not enough of one area to make that a real employable skill. I also live in a city with a poor job market. So, I'm getting concerned that as I get in my 30s it will be even more difficult for me to find a new job should the need arise. Mostly I think it's because I'm unwilling to make the sacrifices to become a life-time employee anywhere, plus I've never found a job that I would be willing to devote that much of my life to.

SPARROW: In the next few years, we will continue to stumble along, I guess. There is a chance that I will become a public school teacher, instructing high school English. I am currently becoming certified in this field (but would rather work more rarely).

CHRISTINA MOSES: In the next few years, my finances are going to increase, double, and continue to do so. I am learning so much as I grow older (and make mistakes) about how to manage my money. I am planting seeds right now where I will be very financially secure.

TIM WISE: I expect to be pretty financially independent within the next five years: debt free, comfortable, with savings: all the stuff I never thought I would be able to say actually. It's sorta nuts in many ways, but I've been very fortunate.

RACHEL MORIELLO: Now that I am more sober in the area of money, I expect my situation to get increasingly better over the next several years—of course, I have always thought this and it hasn't really happened. I really struggle with this issue. How do I make enough money to do what I love to do and be free from the things I don't love to do? How do I have enough energy and time for my creative work? Right now I work three different jobs: I teach after-school twice a week, I teach a Saturday Girl Scout program, and I wait tables four nights a week. With this as a backdrop, I try to pursue my acting career and rehearse/perform with my group. It's exhausting.

RUSS KICK: I expect that the money from my books, added to payment for my freelance articles, will be able to give me a decent lifestyle (i.e., medical insurance, being able to buy a few books a month) by spring 2003.

JASON KUCSMA: In the next five years, I can only hope that we have made *Clamor* a self-sustaining project that will be paying our bills and hopefully branching out into other important media work. As long as I am involved in creating independent media in some way or other, I will be content. It's taken a long time for me to realize where I feel my talents can best be used to help others and possibly instigate positive social/political change, and I want to stick with it as long as I feel I am making a positive contribution to such efforts.

A.D. NAUMAN: I remember once reading about Kafka's life, and how he had a municipal job with short hours and high pay, which enabled him to do a lot of writing. I'm still envious of that. Though I'm not lucky enough to have such a job, I've discovered something pretty useful, and completely by accident: if you find yourself a niche as a freelance writer—say, a medical writer, technical writer, legal writer—you can do pretty well. The pay is not awful and, as a freelancer, you have control over your time. My niche was (and is) as a medical abstractor. I think there are about 20 of us total in the country. At the age of twenty-three, I got a job as copyeditor in a medical publishing company in St. Louis, and though I fled after two years, I kept freelancing and accumulating medical knowledge, which qualified me to do the medical writing. I still do the medical abstracting because, though I'm now employed full-time as a college professor, I do not earn enough to make ends meet.

MICKEY Z.: While I continue to hope that my writing income will drastically increase, I expect more of the same. I also expect that Michele will need a break and I'll have to work more and write less. Then again, things aren't exactly looking up for many people.

I've been rich and I've been poor. Believe me, rich is better.
—MAE WEST

WAKE-UP CALL

(TURNING POINTS, EPIPHANIES)

TIM WISE: In the wake of the anti-David Duke work, there was little remaining question as to the work I had to do, or felt as though I needed to do. Seeing 60 percent of your fellow whites (in this case, in Louisiana) vote for someone who is a devout Nazi, knowing full well who and what he was, has an amazing capacity for focusing one's attention on things. After that, I knew that I had to be involved in doing antiracism work, especially in the white community. I could never take a regular job or career path, so long as this sickness was so widespread in my community.

SUSANA SANTIZO: I knew since the beginning that I wouldn't have a regular 9 to 5. I would tell my Mami that I would be a doctor so she could be happy, then in the same breath told my Papi I would rather be a sheep herder in Peru. I loved the thought of having infinite amounts of wool.

SETH ASHER: One turning point was getting away from cars and more involved with bicycling. There are so many principles involved with bicycling that to me are philosophical and central to societal issues: for instance the social aspect, of not being cut off and wrapped around in steel and glass, but actually being out there in a more natural setting accessible to everyone else. This seems to me to make us feel more connected and helps us think about the consequences of our actions. The self-reliance: getting around on one's own steam. The peacefulness and tranquility: nobody has to go to war to protect cheap oil. Nobody has to steal Native American land to build more highways. If we didn't have all these roadways, you could solve the housing problem. It must be as much as half of our cities that are given over to roadways, highways, driveways, garages, parking lots, gas stations, car washes, dealerships, repair shops, etc. We could solve the housing space shortage. Instead of a roadway in front of every street, what if we had a garden and a plaza and a public square? We have the potential to actualize this vision.

INDIO: It all started when I became homeless 'n began to realize that the system was geared to make you fail, especially for homeless people. The intake workers have a stereotyped concept that we are losers 'n just lazy. The workers are brain-trained to be negative 'n almost push u into a feelin' of wantin' to die or commit a crime so that you are able to get 3 hots 'n a cot in prison 'n just become a ward of the state.

RACHEL F.: I began as a teenager approaching career outside of the "mainstream". I graduated high school knowing I would attend the American Academy of Dramatic Arts, rather than go on to university. The need to support my theatre pursuits and myself led me into "mainstream's" mediocre-level offerings, which I was later able to flip inside out again, using those skills to arrange my freedom and autonomy. I don't think I could ever go back now.

SPARROW: My big mistake in life was reading Lao Tsu's *Tao Te Ching* when I was 12. Suddenly I decided: "I do not want to be a doctor. I want to be...a humble servant." (I saw a mental image of a monk at the doorway of his mountain hut, sweeping the floor.) Ever since then, I have had some semi-unskilled job.

MARTA RUSSELL: When I went from being a walking person to using a wheelchair most everything flipped in my life. I had managed to get jobs as a walking crip but the wheelchair was a turn off to potential employers. I was not the "normal" employee—whatever "normal" means. I did not fit the mode and I soon figured out that there was discrimination out there, big time. Here I was the same person as before, just now using a wheelchair to get around but I was treated entirely differently. My worth shrank. I know that potential employers saw me as a liability. I figured: Why bother?

MICKEY Z.: By 1984, I had convinced myself that I could get a mainstream job and pursue my creative work on the side. So, perhaps influenced by my Dad's law enforcement connections, I actually took the test for the NYPD. My idea was to become the self-defense instructor in the police academy and bide my time until I hit it big with a script or whatever. Well, the NYPD accepted me and asked me to start at the academy in the January 1985 class. At the same time, I got a call from legendary martial artist Leo Fong asking me if I wanted to appear in a chop-socky flick with him and a pre-Tae Bo Billy Blanks in California. To do so would mean that I couldn't start in the police academy and thus forfeit my spot. I thought about it for maybe thirty seconds and chose the karate movie.

RICHARD MILLER: It was in fifth grade that a certain fanatical teacher taught me a thorough disrespect for organized religion by insisting on morning prayers in public school. This man was a sort of Ichibod Crane who clearly didn't like kids. I slashed the tires on his moped and got suspended at the end of the year. It still feels good. In middle school (grades 6-8) I learned to be more quiet, and got my first job. I had a paper route. It was during this period of my life that I started to be more selective about whom I spent my time with. I began to hang around with outsiders. Ronald Reagan was President; the world was beginning to spin further to the right. High School was perhaps the most important time in my life for learning lessons about the ways of people, especially "authority figures." Most of my friends were involved in activities, which landed them under police investigation, or in detention. I myself was regularly questioned about and accused of being involved in petty consensual crimes. Can you say "pot smoking"? I received an early diploma from high school, a gift from an eager staff, along with an official request to stay off campus forever.

GREG RAPAPORT: That probably occurred the first time I went to college. I was majoring in accounting and recreational drug abuse. I attended college in the mid-late 80's and at that time materialism was running rampant. Competition was fierce between students and support was shamefully low. At that time I also found that I definitely had problems with authoritative figures and knew that "kissing ass" was not going to be one of my strong points.

GARY BADDELEY: I suppose I did decide at one point, shortly after I turned 30, that if I was ever going to have the balls to give up the safety of working for someone else it had better be now, before I got weighed down with all the stuff that a good wage would inevitably bring: mortgage, kids, etc.

RACHEL MORIELLO: I think I finally realized that about three years ago, and living with myself has been much easier since then. I had been dating someone and I really wanted to get married. I had really struggled for years with comparing myself to people I grew up with, trying to find "acceptable" things to tell my family about my life, wanting them to think I was "normal" somehow. Right after my break-up, I went upstate (where I'm from) to a baby shower for one of my friends from high school. It was there that it struck me: OH I'M NOT LIKE EVERYONE ELSE! AND I'M NEVER GOING TO BE! Followed by a great sigh of RELIEF and a total loosening into myself! At that party, I didn't even try to play the "normal" game. I thought to myself: *From here on in, you're allowed to be as wild and creative and free as you are; there's no longer any such thing as "normal" in my life!*

JEN ANGEL: Well, I don't know if there was an exact point, but in the last couple of years, I've just noticed that I've taken such a different path from others. My twin sister, for example, works at corporation and makes like 60K a year. I make about 20K at the most. Sometimes I think that if I had taken that path, I wouldn't be having the financial difficulty I'm having now. Of course, I wouldn't have been able to do all of the fun things along the way that I have done.

PANAYIOTA PHAROS: I joined TVI Studios (which is a really great resource for actors) and have been taking acting courses there. It's been a really wonderful, but expensive experience so far. Between headshots, resumes, classes, books, and everything that goes with it, the amount of money I've spent is in the thousands (not *many* thousands—I did say I was a bartender, right??). Its all been worth it though. The amount of experience I've received and the things I've learned have truly been a blessing. However, because I didn't have a steady source of income, the stress and pressure I put on myself to "make it" has been enormous. Every time I'd have a scene or a monologue due for class, I would get so nervous over my performance. I felt that I needed that "oscar-worthy" moment in order to feel good about what I was doing. It took the fun out of acting. I felt slightly inferior to my other more "successful" friends and put this insane pressure on myself. My performances *had* to be great. I *had* to hear that I was doing a marvelous job. Otherwise, what the hell was I doing? Making shit money with a college degree AND really *sucking* at what I wanted to make into my life! I didn't feel good about it and I hated the way I felt about myself. Now this all really happened just recently. I was really depressed about the way my life was turning out. Yes, I was living "the dream" but I was miserable. Wasn't it supposed to be fun? Wasn't I supposed to feel all my stress go away when I got on stage? You know, your spirit becoming one with the character and all the stresses and problems of your daily life fade into the background? I was doing a lot of soul-searching, especially when the office (dating service) closed. What the hell was I going to do? Get another meaningless job and pretend like I am happy living the way I am?

SETH ASHER: Sometime around 1994 or 1995 (I think it was one of those summers) I read George H. Smith's book *Atheism: The Case Against God.* I had stumbled into this title at a bookstore café in Washington D.C. While not previously exposed to atheism in a significant way, Mr. Smith's clear concepts made perfect sense to me. I immediately related to and accepted his beautiful ideas. Atheism is an incredibly liberating concept. It dispels the notion of this great historical falsehood and it clears the air. It creates a positive setting for a positive program. Okay, there's no false code to constrict us by so now we can create an ethical program. How do we live happily? How do all living things ethically co-exist? Instead of relying on this pretended being to do it for us, no, we're responsible! We have to think about the consequences of our actions. We can't rely on an illogical and murderous book (the 5 books of Moses are filled with murderous teachings) to teach us morality unless we accept that: a man and woman can only find sexual fulfillment inside of marriage or that homosexuality is an "abomination." Or unless we accept that the children of Israel are "the chosen people;" or that women are unholy when menstruating and can't be touched in their unclean state and therefore are unfit for many occupations; or that those that don't believe in god or the sabbath or animal sacrifice should be stoned or burned or strangled to death, or that slavery is a workable institution provided the many and detailed biblical guidelines are followed; and on and on and on. All that stuff needs to be thrown out now we can create a good world instead of a world full of hatred. We can have passion, not about religion, but about ethics, humanitarianism, humanism and a happy, peaceful, and healthful way to live.

SANDER HICKS: When I first got to high school, I wanted to be the president. Over time, that changed: I wanted to be a punk rocker then I wanted to be a prophet. I started reading philosophy and economics, sometimes in over my head. I was already getting called a Commie by the jocks, so there was no turning back. My development as an independent thinking person who was politically on the left was cemented by a social ostracizing. And that bitter experience only further pushed in the wedge. My freshman dreams of having a Porsche got left in the dust pretty fast. So I graduated from that all-guys Catholic high school already rejecting the Program: the backwardness of the way we interact in a capitalist society, the "love" that is actually possession, emotional slavery, brutal intimidation.

MARTA RUSSELL: What I did was turn to freelance work as a writer and that writing grew into the main work of my life and the most rewarding work. I found that all the experiences which had brought me to writing also fueled the writing. My niche became the socio/economics of disablement. Common Courage Press published my first book in 1998 and I've written many articles, commentaries and academic papers since then on political economy and disablement.

JASON KUCSMA: There was no clear time when I had any type of epiphany, but sometime in college I realized that I didn't have the same motivations behind my schooling that my classmates did. I took a wide range of liberal arts classes, but I also took a number of communication studies classes and some journalism classes where I was surrounded with very career-focused classmates. They all seemed to view college as a means to an end, where I viewed it more as a process—a place where I would voraciously try to accumulate as many different types of knowledge and skills and use them whenever/wherever they would be useful. Having a job that paid me $60k a year was never a priority, but being happy and having a sense of accomplishment without compromising that happiness or my own values has been my motivation for the last five years.

RUSS KICK: It was a gradual progression throughout my 20s. I think the real turning point came when I was 30. I was involved with a fucked-up woman, and—in the haze of clinical depression that had enveloped me—I wanted to marry her, have kids, and get a 9-to-5 salaried position to support us. After almost losing myself, I finally realized what an emotionally abusive succubus she was, and I ditched her. That's when things came into sharp focus. I realized that I didn't want to be a slave to the grind—that I was born to be a writer/editor/disseminator of knowledge—and that's what I need to be even if it means being perpetually broke (or "assed out," as my sister says). I also realized that I never want to get married again (I already had been a husband once before) and that I didn't want to have kids. Talk about being enslaved—raising human beings saps every bit of time, energy, and money you have. I'd rather put all those resources into my life's work.

MICKEY Z.: One last note on the movie that changed my life: It was called *Low Blow*. Billy Blanks and I went out to Stockton, California, together to work on a project with a lunch budget that rarely went above the peanut butter and jelly sandwich level. Regardless, I did have fun with Billy. We worked out, gave a local seminar, and I even ended up lending him some cash when he ran out. Today, as I watch him prevaricate about both his age and commitment to family values while playing the devout Christian card in the name of exploiting foolhardy consumers and celebrities alike, I have only one thing to say: *Billy Blanks owes me $150.*

SPARROW: When I was 40, I had a kind of mental collapse. Later, I felt the cause was this:

1) I had always imagined that at age 40, I would quit my bohemian youth, and become a professor somewhere. I would begin to wear suit jackets, and have long, helpful conversations with students.

2) Now I was that age, and I was no closer to professoring.

3) In fact, I really didn't want to be a professor.

4) I had always seen my life as a kind of prelude to another, better life—a life my parents might respect. Suddenly I knew my life WAS not a preparation; my life was real. The decisions I had made were, ultimately, final.

5) Also, I had never really achieved success as a writer. I was a failure.

6) Why did I keep pursuing a pointless goal? Why did I ENJOY this pursuit?

7) If a fisherman fishes for 23 years, and never catches anything, he stops fishing.

8) At some point, I had to admit my parents were right, and I was wrong.

9) Either that, or I had to admit they are wrong, and I was right.

10) I could not accept either choice 8 or 9.

Eventually, I decided: "Fuck all success! I will survive as a militant failure!" Soon after that, I launched an attack at *The New Yorker*, which led to my international fame.

I try my best to be just like I am but everybody wants you to be just like them; they say sing while you slave and I just get bored.
—BOB DYLAN

IN MY LIFE

**HOW HAS YOUR CHOICE TO BECOME AN ARTIST AND/OR
ACTIVIST AFFECTED ANY OF THE FOLLOWING AREAS?**

**LOVE LIFE
SEX LIFE
FAMILY
LIVING SITUATION
SOCIAL LIFE
CLOTHES
EATING HABITS
HEALTH
EDUCATION
LEGAL ISSUES**

LOVE LIFE

GREG RAPAPORT: I have a beautiful wife and a great son who wants to play the guitar like his dad.

MARTA RUSSELL: Trying to have a relationship with someone who does not share my politics has proved to be impossible.

SANDER HICKS: God, this is personal. My love life is kind of non-existent right now, but I can't really blame my artist/activist career for that.

A.D. NAUMAN: Underlying everything I had always done and every decision I had always made was the relentless, almost frenzied desire to write fiction. I would not tolerate threats to my fiction writing. The security of the abstracting also enabled me to write fiction, and the man I finally did marry was my major source of writing collaboration. Tim and I passed long evenings talking about fiction writing: narrative voice, plot, metaphor, character development, everything. He and I respected and influenced each other's work. (The year after I won the Illinois Arts Council Award for Literature, Tim won it. I always loved his writing.) Tim was a burly redhead of 100 percent Irish descent. He is not *the* Tim O'Brien, but he's a Tim O'Brien, whose amazing dry wit made me laugh more than anyone else I knew or have known since. I loved Tim deeply, and at the age of thirty-two, I made a decision that did threaten my fiction writing: I got pregnant.

MANNY SIVERIO: My love for mambo dancing was the reason I met my wife. It's the reason why we work together so much and collaborate with artist performance work (as dancers/performers).

CHRISTINA MOSES: My girlfriend is an artist as well and we support and nurture each other through the process.

SETH ASHER: You could say that I lead a rather particular type of lifestyle. An atheist, anarchist, anti-consumer, vegan raw-fooder, cyclist, I am somewhat of a counter-culturist. This means that it can be harder to find common ground with others, most importantly for me, unattached, sexy, smart and likeable women living in my area. But, so what? In many ways I can relate to people that live very differently from me. So, what I consider critical in a partner is genuine respect for the choices I have made and an open mind.

GEORGIA GIANNIKOURIS: I have a big fear of getting into an emotional relationship with someone. I never wanted a boyfriend (which explains why my first real boyfriend came at 20), because I never wanted to be distracted in any way from the things I want to accomplish. I'm constantly cooking up ideas, creating, planning, making lists, and enjoying it all, that I'm always scared to let anyone into this little world. I always thought it would be a bad idea, but after experiencing it I realized it could be a real asset. It helps a lot to have someone you care about being there with you. But I also stopped writing, and that wasn't a good thing. All that energy that comes from too much time spent alone and too many bottled crazy thoughts that only you understand, is suddenly gone because you have someone to share all your thoughts with and to feel peaceful with. It's a very beautiful thing, but I think some of the best work and accomplishments come from being alone and totally focused. I'm sure my mind will change. And the word "love" is my favorite word, after all. Then there's the fear of being too caught up in love that you start to think that all these plans you have don't really matter anymore, or you start morphing to the other person. Or the fact that you meet their parents and you're a nightmare because you're not planning to be a lawyer or a doctor or a good schoolteacher. I'm Greek, it's tough.

TIM WISE: No real effect. I am married to a wonderful woman who is supportive, though not particularly political. And prior to meeting her, all of my successful relationships were with women who were less political than me, but who ultimately shared my basic values of course. For me, political relationships are a pain in the ass: all about ideology and being so wrapped up in one's political/radical persona, that everything else gets pushed aside. And there is more to a person than that, after all.

MICKEY Z.: Since Michele and I evolved away from the mainstream together, my radical beliefs aren't as big an obstacle as they could be for a single activist trying to meet a partner. Still, we don't always see eye-to-eye.

PAMELA RICE: I'm married and my wonderful husband has gone along encouragingly with my work. He also became a vegan, over time, with me bringing a lot of convincing literature into our home.

SUSANA SANTIZO: I always attract a certain type of guy: older, conservative, and close-minded. I am very free with my words, I say what I really feel and usually not what they want to hear. I spend most of the night defending my beliefs, I never get to the second date.

RACHEL MORIELLO: I'm working or rehearsing all the time so it's hard to find relaxation/fun-time for me and my partner (who is also an actor/performance artist/comedian). I have really only been able to date other artists because no one else could understand the lifestyle.

SEX LIFE

MARTA RUSSELL: A partner must not be hung up about disability.

SANDER HICKS: I do occasionally blunder into things and then it's hard to extricate. As I have gotten older, I've gotten more careful. But you know, there are assumptions people make that are just not true, even though you want them to be. Like when White Collar Crime went out and did 5 dates on the Warped Tour with DIY Fest—people in the music industry were like, "Oh you'll definitely get laid a lot." I was like "Do you really think so?" But then when the tour actually happened, it was just a lot of traveling and playing in the hot sun. No one seemed all that horny or available. Everyone was just focused on driving, playing music, smoking herb in the van, and talking about, but never having, sex.

RACHEL MORIELLO: I'm sorry to say much of the time I don't have the energy for sex!

TIM WISE: Well, being a radical activist doesn't exactly get one laid in mass quantities, if that's what you mean. I mean, being a lecturer/writer and traveling around being the center of attention naturally gets you a certain kind of following. And occasionally I get hit on by folks who are sorta like radical activist groupies, and the like. But that's pretty rare. And of course, I haven't reciprocated any of that since I met my wife. Most of the people you meet who are into this kinda thing are pretty substantive people, so they are more likely to want to sit and talk with you, than to sleep with you, hook up, or anything like that.

GREG RAPAPORT: I'm married, what's sex? (Just kidding.)

SUSANA SANTIZO: I never make it to the second date, least of all his bed.

INDIO: Too tired most of the time 'n I got a lot of back pain anyway.

FAMILY

PANAYIOTA PHAROS: I come from a bit of a traditional family. We don't become artists in my family. Especially being a woman! Having to choose a career where I'll have the time to raise a litter and wash dishes and cook for my adoring husband. Like teaching. I was encouraged so much to become a teacher. "What a grrrrreat career for a woman" they all said. It's true. It is. But it wasn't for me—although that was my original major at Hunter. Luckily the system sucked so much in that school (huge pain in the ass to declare your teaching major there) that I decided to say fuck it (partially out of laziness too) and just finish with a plain old Literature degree. And then I graduated and had no idea what the hell to do. How does one become an actor? They still seemed like a special breed of people but I decided to do it anyway. What did I have to lose?

TIM WISE: It makes me a better father I think, and I think being a dad is making me a better writer and activist: it gives me new purpose and a sense of urgency.

A.D. NAUMAN: Ah, babies. They look so picturesque, from a distance. They're so cute and cuddly. You find out that they nap for four to six hours a day, then require twelve hours of sleep at night. You start thinking, "Well, I can write while the baby is sleeping." In fact, when the baby is sleeping, you too are sleeping, because you are exhausted from taking care of the baby. Or, you're doing laundry: this frightening unending pile of laundry generated by the baby. Or you're washing bottles, or picking up toys, or changing the sheets on the crib. In my case, I was also doing abstracts, starting my dissertation, and trying to work on another novel. Then the baby wakes up. The baby, it turns out, is an amazing non-napping baby. The baby is in fact awake most of the time. Half her waking time is spent feeding her. Then there's the trauma of trying to burp her; then you spend an inordinate amount of time trying to get her to take a nap. Which she doesn't do. You don't get angry at the baby—she's so picturesque. She sits around in fuzzy pink clothes, with her fuzzy little patch of blonde hair, and just looks cute. She has somehow mastered looking cute—with big blue surprised eyes and cheeks the size of a nut-collecting squirrel's. No, you're not mad at the baby; you're mad at the laundry, the work, your spouse, your life. For the first time in my life I felt in danger of losing my fiction writing, and I fell apart. But the rest of this story is under the "Regrets" section.

SUSANA SANTIZO: My family is very old-fashioned. My decision to never get married or eat red meat is a constant battle in my house. My Papi wishes I wasn't so blunt and my Mami wishes I could be less aggressive. I think those are my best qualities.

SANDER HICKS: My parents say I'm crazy to my face, but I hear from others that they speak highly of me when I'm not around.

CHRISTINA MOSES: I am supported by my family; they believe in me and encourage me to be true to my dreams.

MANNY SIVERIO: I have a very weird and hectic work schedule that can change at a moment's notice. Plus, by getting married I picked up a family that I didn't have before. It's a matter of learning how to juggle all these responsibilities and being able to communicate better with your spouse so that we can play tag team and pass the ball to the other person.

GREG RAPAPORT: My family doesn't understand my music or passion for it, but they are supportive of it.

SPARROW: I have been in the band Foamola for eleven years. I am one of the singers, and write lyrics to the songs. Also I play the ocarina. Our band is considered humorous, chaotic, familial. My wife and daughter also inhabit the band.

RACHEL MORIELLO: I don't see my family or talk to them very much. Holidays are about it.

MICKEY Z.: My parents support me unconditionally and always have, but I have an uncle who disowned me after 9/11 (don't worry, he's done it before). Also, my older sister and I have grown more distant in direct proportion to the development of my radical views (although I sense a thawing in progress).

GEORGIA GIANNIKOURIS: Being the black sheep in the family has its ups and downs. I know my family worries extra for me. They want to see me settled and happy, and they tend to wish secretly that I could be doing *anything* else. Luckily, they've been very, very supportive of everything I've wanted to do, but I know they're scared. Plus, I come from a Greek family, which is a whole thing in itself. My grandmother is horrified that I'm not married yet, (or have no prospect for that matter), and my grandfather thinks that going to school strips us of the knowledge of housekeeping that is not only essential, but the most important thing in a woman's life. They play matchmaker more often than anyone would like, (and they think they're so discreet about it, too), and they insist that teaching is the one and only valuable job a woman can have. More so, they came to America with virtually nothing, and built an entire family. They have five children and twelve grandchildren and they began working here for fifty cents an hour. At 63 my grandma just retired, and at 73, my grandpa still works, and refuses to stop. So, they don't understand the concept of going to years and years of school, and having these insane passions. They believe in good hard work, two months vacation, and a large family. The thing is, they work this hard to give us the world. My father works twenty hours a day, waking up at 3 AM, working as hard as humanly possible, with every ounce of love for us. After everything they sacrifice and give up for us, *we* want to do better for ourselves. So, when I decide to follow a route that may not have sure results, they feel that I, who have everything, am giving it all up. This can be hard to swallow, and I'd hate for my family to think that I wasn't making the best of my abilities. For example, I love math and it is a very strong subject for me, but I could never go into accounting. I used to wonder why I couldn't just like to do these more "practical" things. But this world would be so bland if we all did that. There are people who hold this world up, and there are people who color it and add life to it. Both are equally important. And both must love their role.

MARTA RUSSELL: I have a wonderful daughter and could not ask for more than that.

PAMELA RICE: My husband and I work as a team with the veggie society. It has given us a rich source of meaning in our lives together

LIVING SITUATION

MARTA RUSSELL: Must be accessible to a wheelchair.

TIM WISE: No real effect anymore.

SANDER HICKS: I haven't really gone into this, but I had a great living situation in NYC for a while there; for 5 years I was the super of two buildings in the Lower East Side: 98 and 100 Suffolk Street. I watched the neighborhood evolve and built an office in the basement of 100 Suffolk. So it was a good situation for a while: a free apartment upstairs, a big 4000 square foot basement office downstairs. I even brought in web design companies to design softskull.com in exchange for space. I was a huge wheeler dealer. At the same time, I was a blue collar grunt doing the trash 3 times a week, and sweeping/mopping the floors once or twice a week.

RACHEL MORIELLO: I have definitely moved in with more than one boyfriend prematurely, because we both needed a place and couldn't swing it any other way. Also, my house is permanently chaotic and messy because I am home very infrequently, usually only late at night after I've had a full day and I am too tried to clean.

MICKEY Z.: Michele and I have lived in the same one-bedroom apartment in Astoria for 10 years. Would we like to upgrade a bit? Yes (certainly Michele more than I). But since our neighborhood has recently become "hip" and we don't want to live where we need a car, we've short on options at this juncture—unless I sell a screenplay, I guess.

SUSANA SANTIZO: My family is the most important part of my life. I find it very hard to leave. I've done it before and I loved it but I can get a lot more writing done if I stay home and pay less rent.

GREG RAPAPORT: I live in my own home by Peekskill NY. I'm surviving.

INDIO: I still have my place.

PANAYIOTA PHAROS: I still live with my parents. I don't believe in paying rent unless I have to. It's so expensive too! If I wasn't living at home, I wouldn't have been able to afford even *half* of the things I was doing (like acting classes for one).

SOCIAL LIFE

TIM WISE: Definitely it affects the kind of friends you have. But I have always had just a small coterie of friends anyway. My best friend today has been my best friend for about a quarter-century, so no real effect.

JASON KUCSMA: Love life, sex life, family life, living situation, friends: All of these are intimately connected with the fact that I surround myself with people who are doing wonderful things; be it art, activism, media, etc. They are my friends, lovers, acquaintances, and comrades. I don't know what I would do if I had to rely on my work or neighbors for a social network of people I can relate to or turn to in times of need. I talk about how we are part of an imagined community that is not geographically or ideologically finite, but is instead sprawling, diasporic. That I can think of myself as a member of a community of people who are vibrant, brilliant and hard-working, is something that motivates me daily.

JEN ANGEL: My activism has affected every part of my life. I believe in mutual aid, cooperation, autonomy, etc. This is what drives my activism, my media work, and every aspect of what I do. I'm a vegetarian, I support independent and local businesses, my partner and I own one car together instead of two, I feel weird when I eat in chain restaurants, I participate in community activities, I practice non-monogamy, I have friends all over the country who are doing the same things.

RACHEL MORIELLO: I work with my friends creatively as much as possible, otherwise I don't see them. I have one friend from home and we made a pact to see each other once per month, no matter what. We're doing good, so far.

GREG RAPAPORT: I have very few friends. And that is entirely my fault. The friends that I do have are either old friends from high school who I see very in frequently or people who I play music with. As for a general social life, I have none.

SUSANA SANTIZO: I can honestly say I have very few friends. I think people my age want to have fun and go shopping and meet guys, that's just not me. I like to politic, laugh, have get togethers, and be free. We usually smoke a little and start to freestyle to our own beats and get up and do spoken word or recite our latest work. It's hard to find friends who are truly free. I am social but I keep to myself. It takes a lot for me to get comfortable with people, but I'm still a friendly person.

INDIO: Most of the time, the people I work with are all my friends, brothers 'n sisters.

MARTA RUSSELL: Lost lots of able-bodied friends during my transition but gained radical disabled friends. General social life suffers. Lots of events are not accessible and since I cannot afford $100-$500 price tags to attend political get-togethers, I don't go to them anymore, accessible or not.

GEORGIA GIANNIKOURIS: My friends are amazing. I've met some of the most brilliant and interesting people. Choosing to be an artist/activist, I've come across excellent friends.

RUSS KICK: I like working at home by myself all day, but there is something I miss about working with other people. There's a camaraderie among wage slaves.

PAMELA RICE: Through my activism, I have the best circle of friends I've ever had, by a long shot. My life is veggie events and many close, wonderful friends.

SETH ASHER: Most of my close friends are people I have met within the last four and a half years (post-revolution). But with family members, things can get tough. The level of acceptance needed to be around someone whose lifestyle seems to be so antithetical to some of my important values can be quite challenging. I take on this work, circumspectly though, and it is rewarding.

RACHEL MORIELLO: I don't have much of a social life, but I'm trying to get out and do things at least once a week. Usually it takes the form of either going to a movie or going out with people from my restaurant job after a shift. I love to dance and every time I go dancing it reminds me that I need more pleasure in my life, pure pleasure.

JASON KUCSMA: I definitely don't have what others would see as an active social life. I would love to be able to spend more time with friends, but that often falls to the bottom of the priority list when there is so much work to do.

CLOTHES

TIM WISE: I dress pretty mainstream, truth be told. I've never been into doing the radical uniform thing: looking different as a statement, or anything like that.

SANDER HICKS: I still buy clothes in thrift shops, but another job I've had that I haven't mentioned yet is that I worked as a model in Milan, and that experience taught me a lot about clothes. So I still wear what I want, and sometimes it strikes people as outrageous. But I also have mellowed out about conventional dress. I always want to have one good suit in the closet; you never know when the occasion will call for it. A serious formal date, a formal business occasion like a Soft Skull Board Meeting where you think you are going to have your ass kicked, or a funeral.

SUSANA SANTIZO: I dress down everyday because of my job. If I could choose what to wear it would be worn out jeans with colorful tee shirts and my Quites (handmade sandals from Guatemala—they last forever).

MICKEY Z.: Fortunately, since I've avoided normal jobs, I haven't had to own lots of clothes. As a vegan, I don't wear animal products like leather, fur, silk, down, and so on. I also try not to buy sweatshop-produced clothes but that is becoming increasingly difficult. Ultimately, I prefer used clothes since they don't require further production. These preferences, of course, push me further outside the mainstream and make it nearly impossible for anyone to buy clothes for me.

PAMELA RICE: I used to wear suits with matching bows around my neck. I negotiated subway stairs on high heels and had a drawer full of earrings, makeup, and fragrances. Now, it's fleece tops and casual flats, but I still don the earrings, makeup, and fragrances, because I like such things.

MARTA RUSSELL: Won't wear anything with a designer label on it. I won't be a rolling advertisement for any corporation and I do try to buy union made products whenever possible.

GREG RAPAPORT: I dress the same going to a job, as I would to a gig as I would to a restaurant. Fancy clothing is very overrated.

RACHEL MORIELLO: I love clothes (costumes!) but unfortunately I can't get anywhere near how I would dress if I had a lot of money. I still rock my own style though, mostly made up of thrift store things mixed with basics from cheap stores like H&M (...do I admit that??)

EATING HABITS

RICHARD MILLER: Don't eat animals. This is bad karma; feeding off the suffering of living feeling beings is a negative thing and will produce negative results. Meat eaters are more aggressive, less creative, less sensitive people than vegans and vegetarians. Also, the animal exploiting industries of the world are not just committing mass murder, they pollute the earth, and create a callous environment for those of us with feelings. Plus in general, vegetables and grains are cheaper than meats and cheeses.

TIM WISE: I eat lots, because now I can afford to eat lots. I have to eat lots of crap when I'm on the road, but my diet is not political in any way, shape or form.

RACHEL F.: I'm a vegetarian and an aspiring vegan.

GEORGIA GIANNIKOURIS: I don't eat. Who has time? I forget to all the time.

SETH ASHER: The raw-food-vegan diet, as first taught to me two and a half years ago by my good friend Rob Miller, provides yet an even healthier and more compassionate path. Essentially, this diet gives us our food in a more natural and unadulterated state: simply eat fruits and vegetables, all uncooked, which is how nature provides them. Uncooked produce yields a set of nutrients that is fuller, more intense and better digested and absorbed. Raw is also how every other species living outside of human domination eats. One can also supplement the meals with some nuts and seeds. This diet has been wonderful for me.

JASON KUCSMA: I love to eat. I eat a vegetarian diet and I love to go out to eat. Unfortunately, I can't eat out as much as I would like (because of limited income) but I do indulge whenever possible. It's one of the few ways I treat myself well.

MARTA RUSSELL: Food is a priority. Most of my budget goes to food.

SPARROW: I am a vegetarian, and mostly a vegan. Perhaps once a month, on the average, I have some cheese. At the moment, I do not eat wheat, either (except on rare evenings).

SUSANA SANTIZO: I don't eat red meat or anything that has pork products in it. I fell off for a few months but I just got it together this week. Mind over matter. I just want to be healthier.

RACHEL MORIELLO: On the days when I work at the restaurant, I pretty much only eat there, for free. Other days, I eat a lot of Chinese food and health food stuff— usually one big meal a day with smaller snacks. I used to cook a lot but I don't have much time for that. I hate to admit this but my mother's friend gave me her old microwave. It's the first time I've ever had one and I used to be so against them but I have to say, it makes eating so much easier. I try to use it only as a last resort.

MICKEY Z.: My increased awareness has led directly to becoming a vegan and being a vegan who prefers consuming organic food has merely exaggerated my "outsider" status.

PAMELA RICE: Go veg, that's all I can say.

HEALTH

SETH ASHER: My way of telling Merck Pharmaceuticals to fuck off: daily yoga classes six days, happy lifestyle, friendships and eating nothing but wonderful raw-vegan food. Ditto for the medical insurers, HMOs, drug stores, clinics and hospitals; none of 'em get my business. Oh, and the same thing goes for Exxon Mobil and company, the motor vehicle manufacturers and related car and SUV businesses and their engendered sprawling strip malls.

TIM WISE: I'm emotionally much healthier, but because the writing is pretty sedentary, and I eat so much crap on the road, I could definitely improve my physical health, drop 30 pounds, etc.

RACHEL F.: When I was in school, one of my rules for myself was to never set an alarm clock. This was one component of the plan to recover my health. Once I felt the energy I had—energy that lasted all day, I came to believe that alarm clocks, and working full time, were completely unnatural. Our very bodies are meant to be well rested, to nap when we're tired, to not be sedentary at a desk all day, and to do a variety of activities and physical motions in a day.

GREG RAPAPORT: Health is important no matter what you do. I run 5 miles, 4 times a week. I also have developed a lot of musician related injuries such as cubital tunnel syndrome, thoracic outlet syndrome and assorted tendon and ligament stuff. These injuries have been difficult to deal with in that they obviously affect my abilities. This in turn can lead to some fairly serious depression. Not Fun.

JASON KUCSMA: I am fortunate to share health care benefits with my partner. It's one of the things I am thankful for everyday. As an asthmatic who also has a lot of allergies, I am very conscious of the status of my health all the time.

GEORGIA GIANNIKOURIS: I think I am just mentally healthy. I feel extremely content with life and I am happy with my decisions. This is such a valuable feeling. All people suffer at some point in their lives of sadness or depression, and to finally feel content is priceless.

MICKEY Z.: The more I've learned about Western medicine and the standard American diet, the further I moved away from these accepted paradigms. Consequently, while most question my sanity, my overall health is as good as can be expected on a polluted planet.

SUSANA SANTIZO: I never ate junk food until I started working at Steppingstone. I am now a recovering addict. I don't exercise except for walking: it clears my head.

SPARROW: I do yoga every day, meditate twice a day, walk (without pausing) for 20 minutes a day; also I perform physical therapy exercises each afternoon. I take a hot bath daily. My meditation group is the Ananda Marga Society.

SANDER HICKS: I was a vegetarian for the first three years that I was a serious radical, but I am no longer anti-meat. I just don't like animals that much, let's face it. I am definitely an omnivore, in so many ways. Aggression has its place in the range of human dynamics.

PAMELA RICE: I feel better than I did when I was a meat eater, 11 years later!

RACHEL MORIELLO: I'm tired a lot and I drink a lot of coffee. I'm trying to work on this.

INDIO: I get a lot of senior moments.

EDUCATION

MANNY SIVERIO: Getting more into film directing has caused me to read books on directing, video, editing, etc.

RACHEL F.: In school I had classmates who studied on top of full-time work, and had families too. I admired their resolve, but they were exhausted and had no social lives. With my schedule of part-time school and work, I truly enjoyed the six years it took to earn my degree.

MICKEY Z.: I decided early on that I wouldn't be paying off student loans for the rest of my life and I'm not ashamed to admit that I really get a kick out of people being stunned when they find out I didn't go to college.

PANAYIOTA PHAROS: College was the first time I was around people who wanted to dedicate the rest of their lives to the "craft" (that word can sound sooo pretentious!). I never imagined people striving to be actors. I always pictured people who became or were actors as a special breed—not for ordinary people like me. The more I got involved in it, the more I enjoyed it. I soaked it up. I wanted to take the hardest teachers with the scariest reputations because I wanted to be challenged. I wanted someone to tell me that I sucked. I needed that kick in the ass because a lot of teachers were and are afraid to tell you the truth. But being nice wasn't going to help me. So I registered for this Classical Acting class taught by one Professor Mira Felner. I had heard that she was really serious about it and really harsh with people. I was scared to death but I couldn't wait to begin her course. The first day that I sat through her introduction, I knew I was going to love her, and I did. She was really sweet but most importantly: she was firm yet fair. She gave everyone a kick in the ass. I still have nightmares of me having to sing lines from *Romeo and Juliet* just so I can understand the fluidity of Shakespeare's words. Utter hell, but it was *exactly* what I needed. I took notes feverishly (and still cherish them). She was tough but when she complimented my work, it was the greatest feeling of accomplishment than I had ever experienced. You knew she meant it and that you earned it. Even with all the acting classes I've taken since then, I still credit her with being a huge influence in my life and for just being good. And not to digress, but I appreciate it more now than I did then because I took her classes in a CUNY school. You hear all these things about NYU (posh posh) and The New School (even more posh posh) and yes, those are great schools. I'm not going to take anything away from them. But there's a certain level of arrogance and complete disregard for the quality of education you can receive at a city school—especially for something in "the arts." It's the like the difference in attitude between people who've grown up in Manhattan's Upper West Side versus *Astoria, Queens*. It feels really good to know that I've taken an ass-kicking acting class with a great professor at a CUNY school.

PAMELA RICE: I know every reason that meat eating is a bad way to go. All of this self-taught!

GEORGIA GIANNIKOURIS: The thing about being in college is that it is more than a full time job. If you opt for higher education, you basically give up a lot of other things. That's why what you do in college should be something you looove. I worked 25 hours a week for my first two years at school. Money must be coming in from somewhere, and it has to be a good source.

SUSANA SANTIZO: My education was that of many ghetto youths: limited. If you were lucky enough you had a teacher who taught you the essentials to survive in the educational system. I wasn't. It seemed like I disgusted my teachers. My questions were unorthodox and I was "too cheerful for someone in my position" (what the fuck was Mrs. Prince talking about?). I was referred to as the Spanish girl and told my hair was "too long for a girl of 6." I knew then my dark skin and long braids were a threat. I spent more time looking outside the window and writing in my marble notebook (example: today Mrs. Tucker only drank three cups of coffee and the bitch keeps falling asleep, wonder if it's really coffee?) then learning the lessons. My teachers ignored me and I was lost. One beautiful day a teacher from pre-K came to the class and asked if anybody would like to spend the day with the kids. My hand was the first one up and my teacher suggestively pointed to me as if to say "yeah, give that girl something to do," I was picked (good thing to, if I saw Mrs. Tucker Fucker pick her nose one more time I would've jumped out the goddamn window!!!)! I spent two years in that pre-K classroom. Everything was perfect, I wasn't a part of my class, my parents were none the wiser (my teachers lied and said I was doing great) and I passed two grades doing nothing. We moved to Long Island and the party was over. While kids my age were learning grammar, math, geography, and all the important ingredients to a good start in school, I was learning that "Milton" could not walk on the line without a buddy and "Rachel" always needed help opening her milk. I had to learn the basics on my own and keep up with the new lessons that seemed to not make sense. I fell way behind just because my school didn't want to pay for teacher assistants and a ticket out the ghetto (MY EDUCATION) was cheaper. I was embarrassed to not know the difference between there and there and that the U.S. was in fact not the whole world. I felt stupid: I just couldn't catch up! I was so busy helping other children and writing I decided to stick with it. I slithered my way through high school and passed by the skin of my teeth (I was a professional bullshit artist; I guess my teachers did teach me something). I was never really there; I was just passing through. English and Art were my favorite, history was important to me because I wanted to see first hand how we were so conveniently hidden away and when I questioned it I always got the same answer "it is not a part of the curriculum." Same shit, different story. I finally graduated and for the first time I felt free! Free of teachers insulting my intelligence, free of the fashion catwalks called hallways, and most of all free from the daily brainwashing I had heard for twelve long, long years. I was forced to be a part of something I could never appreciate not because I didn't want to learn but because I discovered a greater school life. Not the one that they tried to drill in my head but the one I had envisioned staring outside the classroom windows. I didn't think about boys or clothes or parties. I thought about how winter was becoming so warm and summers so cold. The *chuletas* (pork chops) that my Mami had made with such pride made me feel like colon cancer was right around the corner. How I was once considered an alien cause I was born closer to the equator. Makeup was so overrated and I eventually referred to it as a mask for the insecure. Learning about my "self" and people became my obsession the more I observed people and dissected myself the more I wrote. I didn't want to become the girls I saw in the videos or the women I saw on the train getting off on Wall Street, I just wanted to be me. In school I was called the Spanish girl (I went to a predominantly white school), the daydreamer and the high preacher (when I wasn't in class I was in the handball courts smoking weed with my fellow "outsiders" explaining our situation and how there are great things, important things we can be a part of in life and that the answers were hidden inside). I was just being Susana. I couldn't be a part of the rat race not because I want to be different but because I am. I can't compromise my inner self for some Gucci shoes. Life is so much more simple and beautiful than we could ever imagine it to be, but most of us would rather not question the norm for fear of isolation. I learn a lot from people. That is the best education I have ever gotten. Will I go back to school? Yes, but not now. To beat the system you have to infiltrate it.

INDIO: I have 3 masters, D.D., paralegal, arbitrator/mediator, teacher, singer, writer 'n have a PH.D in street-o-logy (the main one to have).

TIM WISE: My politics made going to grad school less appealing, that's for sure, and so I never did.

LEGAL ISSUES

SANDER HICKS: Yeah, legal issues. Soft Skull was sued by people related to the Bush bio *Fortunate Son*, and that taught me a lot about the legal system and the libel laws. It makes me so mad they never had to prove anything, and we didn't ever go to court. Their lawsuit just scared the pants off of our distributor, and that was enough to practically shut us down. It certainly spelled the end of that edition of the book.

PAMELA RICE: I have a great accountant who donates her time to doing the tax form for the non-profit. Happiness is a good accountant. Did I mention that she's in law school?

MANNY SIVERIO: Just when it comes to taxes. I formed my own company and have some one look over all that paperwork which would drive me crazy.

MARTA RUSSELL: I find myself joining as many class action lawsuits against corporations for violations of the ADA as I qualify to do.

RACHEL MORIELLO: I'm in housing court right now. We may get evicted in a few weeks for non-payment of rent. We really fell behind because my boyfriend has had mental illness, I was on unemployment, etc. We've been fighting this thing in court since October. We've been on rent strike because we found out they are over-charging us for our apartment. The people who lived here before us were paying $347/month and when we got the place the rent jumped to $1100. It's a rent-controlled apartment so something is off. At first, it looked like we had a very good case, but we have gotten a lawyer who is now trying to screw us, telling us if we want to win, it's going to take more time and time is money and that we already "owe" him several thousand dollars. He really misled us, and it looks like we're going to have to release him. We go to trial soon, so I don't know what will happen. But over the last few months, I've seen that the court system is anything but fair and just, so I am feeling a little discouraged. It's all a money game.

INDIO: Aware of a lot of criminal, family, jailhouse, 'n street issues-however-still learnin'.

SUSANA SANTIZO: Let's not go there.

I have yet to hear a man ask for advice on how to combine marriage and a career.
—GLORIA STEINHEM

TWO QUESTIONS:

IF YOU COULD BE DOING WHAT YOU REALLY WANT TO BE DOING, WHAT EXACTLY WOULD IT BE?

IF YOU ARE DOING WHAT YOU WANT TO DO, TO WHAT DO YOUR ATTRIBUTE THAT "SUCCESS"?

INDIO: I'd like to have a building that would assist people in need without havin' any ID and would allow them to stay the first month without intake in order for them to ascertain if we could be trusted.

A.D. NAUMAN: Happily, I am doing exactly what I want to be doing. I'm a lucky person: there was a job out there that was perfect for me, and that accommodates my writing; and I managed to realize what it was, prepare for it, and actually get it. "It" is being a college professor. But not an English literature professor: that would bog me down in literature so much I'd forget about other things in the world. I'd turn into one of those writers who only writes about English professors. (I promise never to write a story about a tormented, overly cerebral college professor who finds his youthful passions rekindled by having an affair with a beautiful yet dumb 20-year-old student. That said—every now and then, academics do sneak into my work.) My field is education. I work with teachers, specifically on how to teach kids to read and write. Teachers are very different from writers. They don't have long tragic histories of childhood neglect and abuse, aren't drug addicts, and have not had sex with horses. They actually speak highly of their own parents, wake up in the mornings without hangovers, and don't secretly despise the human race. It's quite inspiring! I love working with these people, and I get to imagine that I'm doing some good in the world: many of my students teach in inner city schools, with all the typical problems, and I help them find ways to better teach their students. The college professor gig is excellent for keeping up the fiction writing—not because you have summers off (you don't), and not because it isn't a lot of work (it is) but because you control your own time. I can find a few hours in the middle of the day to write fiction, which is my best time for writing. Also, though proffing is a lot of work, it doesn't feel like work—it's just fun and interesting. So I never have that god-awful feeling of having the life-force sucked from my body. To what do I attribute this success? Well, to be a college professor, you do have to spend many years languishing in graduate school, then get out and adjunct for a few years, then hope you'll find a full-time job somewhere. I have always attributed any success I've achieved to my frightening German work ethic and a rock-hard determination to never give up. If you simply never give up, eventually you'll achieve something.

MICKEY Z.: I just wanna be "me." When I walk down the street, I don't wanna be considered a shopper or a tourist or a consumer or—most of all—an employee. I wanna be a bold explorer, striving to witness, experience, and discover *everything* within the vast realm of my own unique imagination, curiosity, and creativity. In fact, I don't even wanna be considered a noun. No, I wanna be more like a verb. Far more than any one single thing, I yearn to be sort of an evolving process—a natural resource, if you will. Well, either that, or a minor literary figure. I'm not picky.

MANNY SIVERIO: I'm doing exactly what I want to do which is to work in the film business. I love what I do and been fortunate to do so. The only way I could be more happier is to be able to create and idea, work on developing, direct it and help make it to the final product that an audience will see. I'm currently working on making this a reality. I attribute this to hard work, imagination, and a serious belief in myself. If you believe in yourself, others will see that and believe in you too. This is not being cocky, just being confident.

PANYIOTA PHAROS: In terms of my career, I'd love to host some sort of show to help people or be making movies that change the way people view the world. All the movies that I have seen that I have loved have inspired me because the characters spoke to me. That's how I want people to feel when they see something I'm in. It would be amazing if I had the opportunity to do that. And if people notice my work—that would be even better! Having a family of course is top on my list too. I guess it's what everyone wants, right? Success, love, happiness, and health. Sounds corny, but true.

RUSS KICK: This is it: writing, editing, Web publishing. I'd just like to be making a decent living by doing it.

SUSANA SANTIZO: I wish I could own acres of rich land. Grow my own food and bathe in the waterfall that's behind my house. Every night my family would come over for dinner under the moon and we would sing and tell stories. I would publish all my books but I would never leave my house.

CHAZ MENA: A trade—a fulfilling trade—is one that allows you to develop into a craftsman. This will be accompanied with a profound observation of your mind and body, of your humanity and how it contrasts to participants in other crafts and arts. The work is then a metaphor; as you produce something, other forces are at work (I know I sound awfully Platonic here, but I believe him to be on the mark). You can begin to arrive at ever expansive and resounding truths (folk truths, if you like). I feel that this has not been allowed to me. My understanding is spotted by periods of inactivity.

MARTA RUSSELL: Ironically, my "success" came from my life experience being a disabled person. This has happened to many other disabled persons I know but we are the first generation to turn disability into a reason for pride, not shame; to insist upon rights and resist discrimination; and to agitate for access, to remove barriers to inclusion. We are the first generation to theorize on disablement under capitalism. The Independent Living Movement in the U.S. has provided some jobs for us but we still have a long way to go because private industry and government employers are fighting the hiring and retaining of significantly disabled workers at every juncture of the process.

CHRISTINA MOSES: If I could be doing what I really want to be doing I would be a part of a really great, progressive, challenging, and powerfully creative theatre company. I would be acting on stage and directing plays. I would be doing commercials to earn the money I need to pay off my school loans in full. Commercials and film would also support my theatre career. I would own a photography studio. The work I do there would fund my travels where I would take the pictures I love. My passion is documenting people, cities, villages, neighborhoods, and towns. I would be teaching yoga. Basically, I would be earning a living acting and taking pictures and teaching yoga (creating documentaries comes later).

GARY BADDELEY: I'd like to do what we're doing now, but bigger, better and more of it: making TV programs, publishing books, etc. Plus, we've just optioned an amazing counterculture comic that we want to turn into a movie. I attribute our ability to get this far to our perseverance and to remaining very conservative financially: we don't take on projects unless we can pay for them.

GREG RAPAPORT: I would be writing and recording my twisted brand of music and living off the proceeds. Many equipment manufacturers would endorse me. I also would become involved in other paying musical projects that I would find rewarding.

GEORGIA GIANNIKOURIS: Right now I have to say that I'm where I want to be at this point in my life. I've got big plans ahead and I pray they all eventually work out, but for right now I'm doing what I need to be doing. I'm still in school and it is very important to me, and I'm leaving for Australia really soon—a huge experience in itself that I'm about to go through! But maybe if I were on a huge stage surrounded by lights and soul-lifting music and I was pouring my heart out to the world……hmm….Honestly, I think the most important thing is that I'm driven right now, and I have a formula for getting to where I want to be. I create a plan. Usually this plan consists of many, many lists. Lists are super. They keep me sane and focused. I set deadlines, and check boxes and pinpoint exactly how I'm doing everything step by step. A plan is all I need. Then it's like math—you solve it…figure out a way. You gotta be honest though, and you can't over-calculate and skip steps. Things don't magically appear. These lists must be things that can really work and they could be about anything in the world you wanna accomplish. I also believe you must be a good person, or try your best to be. I mean that. It sounds funny, but if you try your hardest to be a good person and to always act kindly, you are more likely to come out a winner. I don't believe in negativity—I think it deters you from living. Personally I also think that complaining isn't healthy. To be successful in anything you fantasize, you must refrain from lots of complaining, and any self-pity. Money may be tight, and you might feel like you're the one always having trouble in comparison to more established friends. But, be proud of what you've chosen to do. The last two things, are to pray and to dream *huge*. Praying is beautiful and whether you believe or not, it brings about *hope*, which is crucial. And basically if you don't set high enough standards, you'll never actually reach…don't build a short ladder if you want a star—build one that surpasses the sky. If a few rungs break, you'll still be high enough.

SPARROW: Success in work comes when 1) you know what you enjoy and 2) are willing to suffer. If you know what you enjoy, you will find that species of job. But enjoyment is not inevitable; on the awful days you must say: "I accept misery!" Sometimes as a substitute teacher I have hours a day where I can stare at the wall, read issues of *The New Yorker* from 1997, discuss current anime (Japanese cartoons) with teenagers, work on my posture, etc. This is, to me, a successful job.

JEN ANGEL: I would work with media-related projects, and probably be my own boss. Or I would just work part-time and do my own projects the rest of the time. It would be amazing to do media activism during the day and actually have free time at night. Imagine that.

TIM WISE: It was luck. I was in the right place at the right time for the anti-Duke work, and that led to everything since, to be honest. And I wouldn't have been in New Orleans, available to do that job, if it hadn't been for my decision to attend Tulane for college. And I wouldn't have gone to Tulane if I hadn't been chasing a girl, who I had been dating since high school, who was going to LSU. And I wouldn't have ever been dating her if I hadn't met her at a summer workshop for high school debaters. And to be at that workshop required that I first had to become a high school debater. And I wouldn't have done that if I hadn't gotten cut by the baseball team, despite having been an excellent, five-time all-star ball player. And I wouldn't have been cut if I hadn't had a spectacularly bad tryout for some inexplicable reason. So I guess it all goes back to that asshole coach who cut me: and God bless him for that.

RUSS KICK: This doesn't have street credibility, but I have to give *mucho* credit to my parents, who let me live at home during the initial phase of my writing career. I'm not sure how I could've written my first two books while working a "real" job.

MANNY SIVERIO: A big part of my success is helping other Hispanics break into the industry. It used to be an oddity to see Hispanics on a movie set. Now it's reached the point where, on some sets, I speak more Spanish than English. In one case, everyone but the Assistant Director was Hispanic and he was always complaining about not understanding us. I told him, "Hey man, this is America, speak Spanish."

RACHEL F.: I'm almost always excited to arrive at work, because it's challenging without being stressful, it has some routine, but with enough variety that it's not tedious. It's a great blend. Flexibility and autonomy are most important to me, and I think best suited for my own personality. I have found a great job that provides these, so I feel very lucky.

MICKEY Z.: Any success I've had has been the result of having time to work and I've had that time—at different points of my life—because I was living either with my parents or Michele and they helped me enormously. I hate to think where I'd be without them.

PAMELA RICE: I am doing exactly what I want these days, and I attribute this to my husband who, bless him, believes in me and the cause I have dedicated my life.

JASON KUCSMA: If I could continue the work I am doing with independent media in a way that is paying my bills and maintaining my fairly simple lifestyle, I would be more than content. So I guess I'm kind of on the cusp right now of being exactly where I want to be on one hand with one foot still in the day job work that I need to keep to pay the bills. Projecting into the future, if *Clamor* does become something that pays us to work on it, it will definitely be a result of my willingness to work 18-hour days on the magazine for long periods of time. It's a lot of work, but a lot more rewarding than the same amount of work being done for someone else.

A lot of fellows nowadays have a B.A., M.D., or Ph.D. Unfortunately, they don't have a J.O.B.
—FATS DOMINO

IF I HAD A HAMMER

(WHICH TOOLS DO YOU USE?)

SANDER HICKS: I like to keep an open mind, absorb new materials, and then find a way to use them in a way they weren't originally intended. Which is fine, the ideas or the materials don't mind. It's the nature of art and philosophy to be somewhat elastic—there's a gap between creator and created.

CHAZ MENA: That which I can do: work on my craft:
Acting classes with a Master actor
Reading newest literature on the craft
Collating my notes/keeping true to my journal
Seeing new plays
Working on theater workshops (no pay here)
Continuing my regimen of voice and body exercises

PAMELA RICE: Page-layout programs, database entry, knowledge through reading and writing, understanding, compassion, love, the usual.

MANNY SIVERIO: Might, wit, drive, and my personality. I read and try to keep up to date with new improvements in the field. I rely on technology to communicate with others. In my business it's not always who is the best but rather who get to the contact first. So I'm a tech-geek (cell phone, pager, Internet, fax machine, computer, etc.)

JASON KUCSMA: I'm a compulsive organizer. I clean and organize things until they are "just right." And then I organize them again. It helps to keep me focused while also allowing me time to prioritize things. As we get busier, I feel that my need to stay focused and organized is even more crucial to maintaining the work we do. Like many Americans, I'd be lost without my computer. It would be literally impossible for me to do the things I'm doing right now without having a computer as an available tool (with many tools inside it!).

SUSANA SANTIZO: I don't need much. My thoughts, pen and paper. You could spread knowledge by word of mouth. All that is free.

GARY BADDELEY: No doubt about that one: my mind. I told you that British private education came in handy.

CHRISTINA MOSES: I talk a lot and meet a lot of people who are pursuing things that are important to them and see if we can collaborate and or aid each other. I send out my headshots, try to audition as much as possible, and I practice. I train my body because as an actress it's all I have. My mind, body, and spirit have to be balanced and exercised. I do yoga, pray, mediate. I take acting class-es and I take a lot of pictures and create games for myself to teach myself more about my crafts.

GREG RAPAPORT: I use my past experiences to fuel the passion in my music.

MICKEY Z.: I've evolved from typewriter to word processor to computer. I read voraciously and I scan the Internet daily. Still, my most powerful tools are ques-tions. We have plenty of answers; what we could all use are some new questions.

TIM WISE: A keyboard and a set of vocal cords.

MARTA RUSSELL: I use words as both a weapon and a tool to disabuse people of their conditioned views.

Work is a necessity for man. Man invented the alarm clock.
—PABLO PICASSO

NATURAL ENERGY SOURCES

(WHO INSPIRES YOU?)

GARY BADDELEY: The people who inspire me most are the ones who get off their asses and do something. I'm fairly focused on business, so the people who have inspired me most directly are those whom I've worked with and who built businesses from scratch: Gary Gannaway and Cory Robbins (two very successful entertainment business entrepreneurs in New York).

JASON KUCSMA: The question might be who DOESN'T inspire me. I struggle with a feeling of inadequacy because I see so many people doing amazing work in social justice struggles. And what do I do? I make a magazine and work at a copy shop. Of course that is a simplification, but you get what I mean. Sometimes I feel like I unfairly try to compare myself or the way I live my life to others. It can be pretty debilitating sometimes, but I also try to focus on the kind of inspiration I get from these people. I am inspired by anyone who has created or worked on projects that work to amplify the voices of those left out of the mainstream American discourse—the independent filmmakers, zinesters, community organizers, historians, activists, micro-radio broadcasters, artists, etc.

A.D. NAUMAN: "Inspired" is a big word. I have definitively been inspired by the works of Kafka, Faulkner, Ursula K. LeGuin, Camus, Kundera, Marquez, Patrick White—all writers who were/are willing to take chances, stretch literary conventions. Currently I'm inspired by Alice Munro, whose stories are packed with amazing psychological insight and depth. I find the vast majority of contemporary American authors either very limited, producing paint-by-number pieces according to workshop criteria, or ludicrously self-serving—the great writers writing about how great they are, which they can publish because a celebrity author in this country can publish his laundry list (and get a big ad for it in the *New Yorker*). Except for Ursula LeGuin and Faulkner, all my favorite authors are non-Americans. I also have a passion for nineteenth-century literature.

INDIO: Mother, stepfather, relatives, teachers, priests, ministers, friends (good 'n bad ones), writers, reporters, radio 'n TV 'n most of all, THE GREAT SPIRIT!

GEORGIA GIANNIKOURIS: I am soooooo inspired by life! *People* inspire me *every* day. Morrie Schwartz, Paul Coelho, Oprah Winfrey, Willy Wonka, Flavia, Iyanla Vanzant, my best friend Nick, so many members of my family, so many of my friends, so many teachers and people I've come across, my sixth grade drama teacher Ms. Romano, Panayiota, Mr. Jacobson, some random girl in the street, a character in a movie, Van Gogh, etc. etc. etc.....the list goes ON and ON! Songs inspire me. Movies inspire me. Poems inspire me. The searchers, the music makers, the followers of dreams! Inspiration is the fuel of my heart! My God, what would life be if we weren't constantly being inspired?!!

CHRISTINA MOSES: My inspiration comes from many places. Especially from people I know who do not follow rules and traditional standards of education and work. People who believe in themselves and what they want to do and because their belief is so strong, they fulfill their dreams.

TIM WISE: James Baldwin, because he understood what it means to be white in this culture better than any white person I ever knew. Black folks normally do. My mom, because she raised me pretty much by herself, and busted her ass to help put me through college, all of which required her to do a job that she never really loved, for a company that never appreciated her, and which paid her like crap for twenty-three years.

JEN ANGEL: Lots of people inspire me. I think it is important to surround ourselves with inspiring people—that's how I maintain motivation. I consider myself fortunately because I have met and been friends with some really awesome people throughout my life—all through my life. I was thinking today about this guy that I knew in college who was one of the first friends I had who I really respected and who I learned a lot from. He owned his own business, and really just knew what he wanted. I learned a lot about figuring out what you want out of life and going after it. I have a bunch of really awesome friends. I'm continually inspired by my friend and partner Jason Kucsma. We say that we work on the magazine together, but really he does a lot of it. I work full time, so there's no way that I can carry even a third of the workload. He has a part time job, but I swear, he must work on *Clamor* 16 hours a day. He sleeps like 4 hours a night. He really is the most amazing person I have ever met.

JASON KUCSMA: I'm inspired by my partner, Jen, who works a full time job in a professional situation and then comes home to help out with the magazine. I work really hard to take some of the burden off of her shoulders, but there is still a lot of work to do. She manages it well. A lot of people in her situation would work all day, come home, and watch television, but not Jen. There are nights when she'll come home, have a dinner, and spend the next five hours editing pieces for the next issue.

PAMELA RICE: Karen Davis of United Poultry Concerns (Machapango, VA). I can truly say that she is the greatest person I know alive today. She has, through many brilliant, reasoned arguments made me totally overcome the conventional wisdom (false notions) of our society that says that animals have inferior worth to humans. With domestic poultry as her point of reference, Ms. Davis rises to greatness as she convinces you through airtight logic of the noble stature of "the lowest of the low," as she puts it: the common chicken.

MARTA RUSSELL: Helen Keller inspired me. Not the Helen Keller portrayed in the movie *Miracle Worker* but the real Helen Keller who fought for social justice: "There has never existed a truly free and democratic nation in the world. . . I have entered the fight . . against the economic system under which I live." Helen Keller, socialist, addressing the Women's Peace Party and the Labor Forum in 1916.

GREG RAPAPORT: People who are self-made and who became successful on their own inspire me.

SUSANA SANTIZO: This might sound funny but it was Jesus. I was brought up Catholic and I always heard these amazing stories about the Son of God. I never took the parables literally because I thought it was just a book of knowledge. A man that was the Son of God. He made a blind man see, fed 5000 people with 3 fish and 2 pieces of bread. Fuck Superman.

PANYIOTA PHAROS: Two books by the author Paulo Coelho that have changed my life and have inspired me to continue working towards my dream:
-*The Alchemist*—one of, if not, THE most amazing story I have ever read. Anytime I am in a rut or feeling like crap about my life, I remember that book and immediately feel peace within myself.
-*Veronika Decides to Die*—a story about a woman who, contradictory the title, decides to live. Invigorating. It makes you want and feel like you can conquer the world.

RACHEL MORIELLO: Rick Shapiro, my partner-in-crime, has definitely inspired me the most. He believes in me and saw things in me before I could see them in myself. He encouraged me to honor myself and my creativity, to seek therapy so I could heal from childhood pains, to put myself out there and believe in myself as a performer.

JASON KUCSMA: I'm also really inspired by the work of the Independent Media Centers. We started *Clamor* about the same time that the IMCs started, so we've both grown alongside each other. I wish we had the kind of reach that the IMCs have developed in such a short time.

A.D. NAUMAN: I'm not sure I've been "inspired" by a person in my life. I've certainly be encouraged and positively influenced by peers and a few teachers. However, I came to view myself as a good writer early in my life and simply expected encouragement and praise—arrogant, yes, but it served me well through the lean years. I have also, though, run up against a tremendous tide of discouraging comments—not because of the quality my writing, but because I talked about being a writer. Actually, most people did not even bother to be discouraging; they were just dismissive. Some people even snickered. I hate to say this, Mickey, but mostly it was the men who snickered, were dismissive, and didn't spend another nanosecond of their time bothering with me. On meeting me, they did not believe I could be any kind of a serious writer. I have encountered dozens of these guys, mostly in writing workshops but also among friends. Once I was out with a boyfriend, and we ran into a friend of his. The friend talked about the novel he was writing. (On and on he went.) Then my boyfriend told his friend that I was also writing a novel (*Scorch*). Mind you, I'd known this guy all of 10 minutes. He was a snickerer: he said, "No she's not." My boyfriend said yes, yes, she is. The friend's response was, "Then it's not very good." This didn't happen in medieval times; this was only three years ago—and it was not an uncommon occurrence, it was typical of the response I would get from men, especially male would-be writers. I find this sad, because we might have been colleagues and had good discussions about writing. Instead, these men find it necessary to assert their superiority over me and toss me in the trash. That kind of discouragement, of course, only made me angry and more determined to succeed.

SPARROW: As for what inspires me, I am reading the book *The Return of Martin Guerre*, an exemplary work of true history by Natalie Zemon Davis: deftly researched, direct in prose, suspenseful (Harvard University Press, 1983). I often think of my guru, with his hands pressed together before his chest, saying: "Namaskar," which means...It doesn't matter what it means. The weather inspires me, here in the mountains. At the moment a cold night rain taps the three windows beside me. The weather seems to be speaking to me, almost.

MICKEY Z.: The people in this book.

Maybe you can keep me from ever being happy but you're not gonna stop me from having fun.
—ANI DIFRANCO

CALL 911

(HAS SEPTEMBER 11 AFFECTED YOUR ART, YOUR INCOME, YOUR ACTIVISM, YOUR LIFE?)

MICKEY Z.: I knew a couple of people who died in the WTC.

GARY BADDELEY: I can't really tell so far. If anything, I think it has increased interest in all things "Disinformation." I'm definitely not one of those people who don't want to live in New York anymore (yes, I live downtown), or not ride the subway, or whatever.

JEN ANGEL: Obviously, since I publish a magazine, we've had continuing coverage of how it had affected people's lives. Also, it has brought people together on a local level, though I wish it would have been more of a catalyst. We do live in a small town, however, so it's not like there's this huge mess of radicals waiting to organize around some issue. Also, because of where I worked, we've had to increasingly worry about security issues. Our clinic was one of the 100 or so around the country to receive anthrax hoax letters after 9/11, so that caused some major issues for a while.

GREG RAPAPORT: 9/11 has affected the economy thus it has affected my backlog of work. Pre 9/11 I had a healthy 5-month backlog. Now my backlog is substantially smaller but is growing once again.

SUSANA SANTIZO: It definitely affected everyone. It made me see the true evil in people, crashing a plane into thousands of people, a whole nation believing that the U.S. was the only victim. Have we forgotten the famous saying "an eye for an eye, a tooth for a tooth"? I am in no way implying that anyone deserves to be killed. I am just recognizing the two guilty parties. It also showed me the good in people. Everyone gave something and some gave everything. It was very inspirational.

MICKEY Z.: In terms of income, I had made the decision to try teaching as way to make money and the only place for someone without a degree to teach is in a continuing education program. So, without much effort, I was able to get myself into the West Side Y and LaGuardia Community College and I put a fair amount of work into preparing for the new challenge of teaching four writing classes. However, registration fell smack dab in the middle of the 9/11 aftermath and a total of four people signed up for the courses. They were cancelled, of course, and that directly led to the job working at the corporate gym where I'm currently employed (cue the shame and self-loathing).

RACHEL MORIELLO: It affected my income at the restaurant. People started being much more conservative with their money.

SANDER HICKS: I woke up on the morning of 9/11 with a song about Jim Hatfield, the dead biographer of Bush, on my lips. I wrote that song and kept writing it when Aunt Phyllis came back from the farmer's market with the news. So the 9/11 disaster made it into the third verse of this song. I was not surprised at all that 9/11 happened, not with the way we've been treating the world. And after Jim Hatfield, nothing can really faze me.

CHRISTINE HAMM: It certainly affected my life, but it hasn't percolated through my brain enough yet for me to make any art about it, or even really write about it. I imagine in about a year it will start to appear in my work.

TIM WISE: It has increased demand for my writing and speeches. As for my life in general, it has been very sad of course, and as a new father, our response to the attacks has enraged me: I sincerely fear that my government is laying the groundwork for a much less stable world, and that my daughter will inherit that legacy. So I'm more pissed now.

MARTA RUSSELL: 9/11 has put a serious halt to politics in the U.S. When George W. Bush and Dick Cheney can use "terrorism" to silence dissent from the weak-willed Democrats, that stops progress in a two (one) party corporate state, however small potential progress may be. Bush happily frames the nation at "war," a long war and it is like the citizenry has taken a poison pill of willful ignorance.

This brand of patriotism dulls the mind. Journalism suffers. Lies are told and the corporate press does not investigate or refute them nor does it allow dissent from the ranks. Generally speaking, challenges to capitalism suffer more repression when our capitalist nation is "at war." That cramps activism of all kinds by making it more risky but it also makes activism more important too.

PAMELA RICE: It didn't affect me in any practical sense outside of spending a lot of extra time reading the popular press. I'm pretty morbid to begin with. At least once a day I think about what would happen if for some reason I were to perish suddenly. Now that the threat of New York City being the target of a suitcase-size "dirty" nuclear bomb is a real one, my morbid self is on unusually high alert.

Work is the refuge of people who have nothing better to do.
—OSCAR WILDE

I'VE HAD A FEW

(REGRETS, THAT IS)

TIM WISE: Initially yes, I had regrets, but not so much anymore. The only thing I think I ever have momentary regrets about would be not going to graduate school. Sometimes the white male credentialistic bullshit creeps over me and I begin to doubt my "qualifications" for the work I do, because I don't have an advanced degree. But then I remind myself that the only folks who really place a premium on that kind of thing aren't concerned about social justice in the first place. It's internalized white supremacist thinking, and it's debilitating, so I try and let it go.

MICKEY Z.: Yeah, I wish I'd had cultivated a fallback option so I could've earned some money while I wrote and educated myself. As for my activism and social awareness, my only regret is not waking up sooner.

A.D. NAUMAN: Now that I'm older and looking back, I see pretty clearly what I've given up for writing, and I do have regrets. When I was in my early 20s, I decided I would make any sacrifice for art. And then I did. I spent my time working and not forming deep friendships. You have to choose: Do I sit down at the computer now or call to chat with a friend? Do I spend Saturday afternoon writing or playing softball? Go out or stay in? I had been a very shy child, and it was easier for me at first to forego the social scene to hide in my room and write. As a young adult, I had boyfriends that took up the small amount of free time I had, and I ended up with very few outside friendships. For a long time, this seemed like a fair trade-off—it was, after all, for art—but lately I have begun to feel genuinely lonely. I look around at other people in the world, and they all seem to belong somewhere, they seem to have strong connections to others, and though they may not have lots of money or spouses or children, they have the genuine affection of genuine friends. I suppose it was not just a matter of time not spent; I was always so focused on my writing. All I really wanted to talk about was my writing. I couldn't get interested in the types of things other people talked about (well, except for gossipy love-affair problems—everyone is interested in that). I couldn't really get interested in the latest alderman scandal or sports or TV shows and movies. I must have been a pretty tedious conversationalist. The best times in my life were when I had friends who also wrote, but friends tend to scatter.

GARY BADDELEY: Yeah, of course I've had regrets. Actually, on second thought, it's not so much regret, rather a niggling question that occasionally pops up, along the lines of "I wonder what would have happened if I'd chosen a different path?" Not that I'd choose differently if I could go back in time.

RUSS KICK: No. I might wish that I had money for a dental check-up or subscriptions to a dozen magazines, but I don't regret anything.

SUSANA SANTIZO: None. Everything that I have sacrificed was never in vain. I'm lucky.

SANDER HICKS: I'm trying to think of one. It's a problematic question, because, we, your subjects, are living lives based on that gradual series of choices. They add up to one choice, this all adds up to one life. So the question is really "Do you yourself have regrets?" I'm having a hard time answering this head-on. I'm reminded of talking to my father about his early life, about how he never played sports in high school or college, but one time a soccer expert came to his university, and my dad took the ball off him on the field. He was encouraged to take up soccer, but felt that studying was too important. He said that he often thought would his life have been different, maybe better, if he had tried to play soccer, as well as major in economics? But I was young when I first heard this, and I blurted out, "NO REGRETS! Right?" (I think I was thinking about that song "I Regret Nothing." Which is by some older female Spanish or Italian singer...this vague cultural reference comes somewhere from the 80s, as does this story.) I don't know why I had programmed myself to reject the notion of "having regrets" at so early an age, but I had. I have reflected upon this little anecdote often. I think my dad's response was to say, "Yeah, but...." and then be a little pensive. What he didn't say, which he could have, was "That's bullshit. I do have regrets." Even now, after working through this, I still am tempted to say I have no regrets, that I wouldn't be me if I hadn't made these choices, constructed that company, formed that band, broke up with those women...to the exes I sometimes muse over, I want to say regrets are everywhere when you can feel the pain you've caused, but it wasn't time to settle down and you were not the one.

MARTA RUSSELL: I feel saddened by the fact that my father still after all these years remains unyielding and condemns my politics and me for having them. This has negatively affected our relationship and I would like that not to be my reality. One, however difficult it may be, must be true to one's self, otherwise all is lost. How many would be activists are out there that are held back by family politics?

SPARROW: Yes, I do have regrets about my entire career in "the arts." Like a nun or an invalid I have watched the society from my windowsill, preoccupied with my inner memories. I wish I had DONE some job, or action, or saved a person. But whenever I start to do so, I believe I am neglecting my real purpose.

INDIO: I only regret that I don't have the money that I had when I had my own business because I would be able to do a lot my own way 'n really be able to assist more people. Now I have to eat crow a lot to assist homeless 'n lower-lowers.

A.D. NAUMAN: A sacrifice I made, which may not have been necessary, was foregoing a "normal" family life—you know, with a spouse and a few children—I mean, children actually fathered by the man you're married to. In my mind, and especially as a woman, diapers and Big Wheels and a guy going off to work with a briefcase every morning were completely antithetical to the writing life. I didn't at all see how they could be combined. It was either/or. I was thirty-one when I gave it a try. I married a fellow writer and had a baby. At the time, I was beginning *Scorch* and I was also working to bring in half the family income, trying to finish a doctoral program, doing laundry, picking stuff up off the floor, taking care of the baby, and cleaning up after two aging cats. The work on *Scorch* wasn't going well. My husband and I were fighting almost constantly. Suddenly I saw myself in the kind of life I'd always feared most—an ordinary life, a non-writing life—and so I left. I packed my stuff and half the baby's stuff (I kept half-custody of my daughter) and moved into a one-bedroom apartment in the city. The bedroom was for the baby. I slept, worked, and ate all in the living room. I embarked on a series of disastrous love affairs. I did manage to finish the doctorate, finish the novel, and keep myself relatively sane. I do believe that, without the experience I gained in those hard long years, I would not have written a novel as good as *Scorch*. But I do have regrets—I'll never have a second child, never have the father of my child to share memories with, probably never own a house. I'm missing half my daughter's childhood, which grieves me (It turns out that, once you get past the initial shock of having children, they're amazing fun!) Now, looking back, I wish I'd been more patient and tried harder to find ways to be both a writer *and* a happy person with a husband and children. On the bright side, though, I have another cat, who incidentally is a lot neater with his litter box. He is an enormous all-white cat named Snowball. His name is Snowball because, when it comes to naming cats, I have a shocking lack of imagination.

GREG RAPAPORT: The only sacrifice I made is that I would be making more money and providing better for my family if I went corporate.

JASON KUCSMA: I wouldn't necessarily say that I regret them, but the decisions I have made in my life have thus far made me far from financially stable. Money will always be a source of stress and tension (both for myself and for the magazine). There are times when Jen and I joke about how we wish we had jobs that paid $80-100K a year salary. Of course there is a whole list of compromises that a job like that would entail, but we still joke about it.

PAMELA RICE: No regrets whatsoever, ever. There is nothing I'd rather do with my life but my activism.

RACHEL MORIELLO: I really believe regret is a useless emotion.

Work is a necessary evil to be avoided.
—MARK TWAIN

WHO'S NEXT

(ADVICE)

RICHARD MILLER: If you plan on trying to survive as a creative person in Amerika, people will not make it easy for you. So here are some tips to keeping your balance and individuality in our corporocracy. Smile a lot, I know this sounds silly, but be happy that you're not that miserable bastard in the shirt and tie next to you on the train, in traffic, etc. This is a soulless person more likely than not, and it should make you feel good not to be them.

MICKEY Z.: You don't need a $100 pair of sneakers to "just do it."

SPARROW: The problem with being an artist is that people constantly give you advice. They want you to achieve more than you have achieved, and they possess a plan for this achieving. On the other hand, they take you out to lunch while giving you the advice, which is very kind of them. (Suggest an Indian restaurant.) When you are a young poet, young women will sleep with you. But as you age, young women will no longer sleep with you (because you are old), and middle-aged women are too smart to sleep with you. For this reason, it is wise to get married.

A.D. NAUMAN: The other day my daughter, now eight years old and a die-hard Harry Potter fan, told me that when she grows up she wants to be a famous writer like J.K. Rowling. I had to smile. I told her that's what I had wanted to do. She looked highly confused. I wondered if, at that very moment, J.K. Rowling's daughter, who is the same age as mine, turned to her mother and announced that, when she grows up, she wants to be an obscure writer like A.D. Nauman.

TIM WISE: Do not doubt yourself. Or if you do, let your faith in doing what's right be stronger than your doubt. Take your time. Justice will not likely come in your lifetime, but you can help move us towards that; and that is the most noble task of all. Having to get it all done by next week is the enemy of justice: it encourages burnout and frustration. Be patiently impatient. Be on fire for justice, but remember that fires have to be fed slowly or they tend to flame out. Pace yourself.

MICKEY Z.: You don't need Burger King to "have it your way."

SUSANA SANTIZO: Always follow your heart. It will never fail you.

GREG RAPAPORT: Man, you better love it 'cause you can sustain a lot of damage along the way and not get compensated for it. (Do I sound jaded?)

MARTA RUSSELL: I would not presume to offer anyone any advice!

RUSS KICK: Be prepared for poverty. If you're going to write books, remember that it takes ages for the royalties to kick in, and even then they may not be a whole lot. Also keep in mind that some publishers are simply crooks who will rip you off. The douche bags at Masquerade Books and Carroll & Graf still owe me thousands of dollars from 1996-7 that, as they've made clear, they have no intention of paying.

RACHEL F.: Each person has to decide what's most important to them: money, security, autonomy, free time, health, routine, spontaneity. We start out programmed to some degree or another, making choices we're steered to, or trained to make. It takes time and luck to be able to discover what your preferences are, what really motivates you, and then to arrange things so that these can be honored or lived by.

GARY BADDELEY: Don't quit your day job. Only (half) kidding. The tough part about quitting the rat race and becoming an artist, or whatever, is that even if you have talent, it often takes an inordinate amount of time for anyone to appreciate your talent or, more importantly, for you to be able to make any money from it. There's not much point starving yourself into submission and climbing back onto the rat race ladder but in an even worse position.

MICKEY Z.: Eat when you're hungry and sleep when you're tired.

RACHEL MORIELLO: Money really helps. I don't know what to say about that except try to find a way to make some, doing something you don't feel bad about. No one should have to do something they feel horrible about to support themselves; there are always options, albeit most of them are less than ideal. Also, get an internship or work study position to meet people that are doing the same kinds of things you want to be doing. Learn from example and from DOING and ASK FOR HELP (something I always had a hard time with). Everyone deserves a hand up and you will help someone else along the way!

SETH ASHER: Just think and make your actions line up with your priorities. Don't let them mess you up so that you have one set of beliefs and a whole different lifestyle, with little in common between the two.

RICHARD MILLER: Never take a job with any kind of strict dress code. A company that is obsessed with how you dress will read your mail, listen to your phone calls, monitor your Internet activity and in general will be a part of the problem; if you catch my drift. These are jobs for sheep; leave them for the sheep.

SPARROW: Fame and success are useless. The only value of success and fame is to teach one the worthlessness of fame and success. The most important thing in life is to be goofy, and unserious. Eventually, for anyone, the question is: do you laugh to yourself, on a Tuesday, when you drop your washcloth in the shower?

RICHARD MILLER: Keep only a few close friends. You only need a small amount of friends to be happy. The more people you're close to, the less close you are to any one of them. Remember having unpopular opinions can cause you a lot of stress if you have to worry about "so and so said you thought…" this can be avoided by simply being selective about who you open up to.

RACHEL F.: I believe that most skills people have can be turned into enjoyable income sources. It's vital to do work we enjoy. But if I feel I have freedom within my work, I will be able to enjoy aspects of it, even if other parts are less rewarding. I once went to a workshop on small-scale entrepreneurship. They told us to write down five things we're good at and enjoy. With creative thinking, these could be turned into very small, unique businesses. An example was given of a young man who was able to program VCRs. This task is mystifying for many people, as is reading the manuals. For $45.00, he'd go to your home, and give you a personal lesson in how to program your VCR. There was a market of people who would rather have the process explained to them in this way, which allowed them to better ingest the information. The point was to be creative, and reach out to the right people.

SPARROW: Fight the fuckheads who run the media-corporate-military axis. They are sinister, and do more damage than we imagine. Be nice to everyone (even those fuckheads, if you meet one at a party). Hate is more gruesome than war. Find something great to believe in—some guru or god or princess.

PAMELA RICE: Do one thing, do it better and better each day, do it for the long run. Don't flit from cause to cause, and be touched by an omnipotent being. That last one no person can control.

SPARROW: Shakespeare and Coleridge—and even Spenser—are profound, and worthy. Listen to jazz; this will not be easy, but it is the highest American art. Edna St. Vincent Millay, Langston Hughes, Emily Dickinson, W. H. Auden: study them. Also Robert Louis Stevenson, *The Epic of Gilgamesh*, O. Henry, *Tales of the Arabian Nights*. Movies are almost pointless (unless you are a filmmaker). Walk a lot. Lie abed. Read. Spend hours in any library. Get an easy job where there is time to ponder. (Art is mostly THINKING.) Look for comic books in the garbage. Don't worry that you are a failure. According to Buddha, it's okay to be a failure. Eventually, you will produce what you are destined to produce. Better to be a crappy artist than a brilliant claims adjuster.

MICKEY Z.: Okay, here's a more serious answer. Follow your heart but please cultivate a fallback option. Learn some skills that will enable you to work at lucrative freelance-style gigs and leave ample time for your passions. You can't expect to make a living as an artist or activist but I hope you'll work your ass off to make it happen anyway.

RICHARD MILLER: Never vote republican, or democrat for that matter, but always vote. This is your license to bitch, renew it at every possible opportunity.

MANNY SIVERIO: Be patient. Keep your options open and be ready to take advantage of any opportunities that come your way. By the same token don't burn your bridges. You may never know when you need to go back or need a good referral. Bottom line: never try to hurt anyone to get ahead. I believe in bad karma. What goes around comes around.

RACHEL F.: I think a 25-hour work week is ideal. I think living simply lets us need less, and notice great free things, like concerts in parks, movies at museums, and dance lessons on the piers on summer evenings. We need exercise every day— yes, every day! Shut off the TV, or plan what programs you'll watch. Ask, "Am I spending my time the way I would like?" Pick your favorite cause and volunteer to do something you enjoy at a place where you admire what people are doing, and where you can learn new skills.

SANDER HICKS: Put yourself in top physical condition and stretch often. Eat a lot of protein. Put yourself through little tests: like can you hitchhike the country in less than a week? Can you teach yourself the saxophone? Can you take the bus to Portland? How fast can you learn new things? How do you learn? Do you know?

JASON KUCSMA: I'm still learning how to make it work. I don't know. I guess I would remind someone that if they truly want to be good at something, they should plan on working at it for a long time before seeing any return on it. We can't expect our projects to take off overnight. Sure, that happens for some, but for the rest of us it takes a lot of work.

SPARROW: Remember, the workers who actually do the difficult work of the earth are the ones who deserve our respect.

RUSS KICK: Also brace yourself for comments from friends, family, and acquaintances about your little hobby, which of course isn't a real job, even if it brings in enough money for you to scrape by. In my case, I know people who seem to think that 400-page books just write themselves. Spending ten hours a day (often more) pounding out books and articles isn't *really* work. This attitude can be upsetting, but at the core, they're right. To paraphrase Thomas Edison, if you enjoy what you're doing, it's not work.

RICHARD MILLER: In the words of B. Dylan "It's rough out there, high water's everywhere."

A.D. NAUMAN: I would tell would-be artists this: You are probably already ahead of the game, because you're thinking of what to do to live a meaningful life. Most people appear not to give this much thought: they think of what they can do to make money, then how to spend the money; they use their time on earth making and spending money—acquiring and consuming. The less "ambitious" ones pass time (kill time) sitting in jobs they don't really like, then finding ways to be entertained in their off-hours. So (I would say), congratulations. You are probably more self-aware and more intellectually alive than most of your peers. This is definitely a good thing. But you must understand: You are probably not going to become famous. I know you don't believe me, because you're different, right? You're really talented, and really dedicated, and really special. Well, the truth is, that's what everyone thinks. Truth is, you are really not special. You're subject to the same universal laws as everyone else: odds are you will not be canonized or recognized on the street or showered with adoration and wealth. However (and here's where

I hesitate, uncertain about this myself) perhaps, not in the middle of your life, but at the end of your life, you will look back and see that fame, fortune, and accolades do not matter. What matters is that you have given the time you had on earth to the pursuit of living meaningfully, to shedding some light on this strange and hurtful human existence, to making the world a better place. You have not passed your time on earth simply acquiring as much stuff as possible, staring blankly at a television screen, converting products to garbage, producing junk that no one needs, tricking people out of a buck or two, or letting your intellect and talents rot. The vast majority of us will be little-known artists, stuck in the minor leagues. It's irritating when we note that some of those major-league players really aren't all that good; that it's not strictly talent and ability that assign your place. But, oh well. Maybe the minor leagues will turn out to be enough—just fine; maybe what's important is not where you play but that you play.

Lawyers, doctors, plumbers, they made all the money. Writers? Writers starved. Writers suicided. Writers went mad.
—CHARLES BUKOWSKI

WHY TWENTY-FIRST CENTURY AMERICA NEEDS ARTISTS AND ACTIVISTS?

GEORGIA GIANNIKOURIS: To color it.

MANNY SIVERIO: The more we rely on technology, the more we have to learn to express and rely on human creativity. We shouldn't sit back and let technology do stuff for us. We have to learn how to use it to find new ways to express ourselves. In essence, create new art forms but don't forget about the old arts themselves, i.e. a writer writes, an artist draws, etc.

TIM WISE: Both are needed as harbingers of what is wrong, and what is right about the culture. A civilization needs poets, of all kinds. Without artists, without activists, there is little reflection, little joy, little opportunity to glimpse oneself as one *might* be. Instead we have to settle for how we already are: and that is not always a very encouraging picture.

RACHEL MORIELLO: Now, more than ever, we need artists and activists to question the "norm," to keep minds open and searching, to heal a very sick society that's based on consumerism, commercialism and the war machine.

MARTA RUSSELL: Given the degradation of the environment and the consumption of the planet which is on a collision course with survival, activism is vital as it never was before.

MICKEY Z.: Years ago, I read an interview with Patti Smith in which she compared a poet's role in society to that of Paul Revere. Someone has to ride through the streets yelling: "The British are coming." The artist provides such information without dictating what should be done with it. As for activism, I see it like this: As terrible as conditions are now on Planet Earth, things would be 1000 times worse without the collective work of activists across the globe. If we haven't already past the point of no return, our only hope is well-informed collective action.

SUSANA SANTIZO: I never really thought about that. I would say because we need to be more in tune with our spirituality if we ever want an effective revolution we need to point that out. If one spiritual person can affect a handful of people in a positive way, imagine a handful of spiritual people.

GREG RAPAPORT: Music is a way for people to directly and indirectly express their feelings. People who write "fringe" music have a tendency to be true to their art and show a truer picture of who they really are. Just like every other "medium," music has been corrupted and poisoned by corporate greed and the greed of the artists themselves. Motivation is a key issue. If you create music for the sole purpose of becoming famous and making lots of money, you are perpetuating the degradation of true music and crippling the exploration of new musical direction. If you create music as a form of expression and to challenge yourself as an artist you are then a true artist in your own right. If you try to market your creation through unorthodox channels, turning people on to what you have to say musically, then you are a musical activist.

SANDER HICKS: Because we need to reject the entire program being taught us and we need to teach other a whole new program, a whole new set of values and principles. We need to destroy this oligarchy, this new American imperialism, and create a truly global society based on mutual aid, common interests, justice, peace. Art plays a big part in this. The pen is mightier than the sword, and the mouth is mightier than the pen.

CHRISTINA MOSES: We need artists. Artists fill in the spaces where there is a lack of communication and a lack of realized dreams, aspirations, and goals. Artists are fun (well, we can be) and having fun is necessary. Artists remind people of their own creativity. Artists embellish and strip reality; we tweak it and recreate it. It feels good to create. I believe that there will be a resurgence of art (however broad it is) as something that is necessary and vital in society. As something to do because it feels good—as a way of teaching and learning and assessing society and history. Creativity is organic and will never diminish. Plus, people are in need of getting in touch with creating and fulfilling on what is important to them. Art provides that clearing.

SPARROW: Certainly activists; without them, we are about to descend into a very bland version of Hungarian fascism. As for artists, do we need them? Well, we have them, whether we need them or we don't. Or DO we have artists? At this point, I suspect all we have is entertainment, of various strengths. Take me, for example. I am a type of comedian. If I were funnier, I could actually make $50,000 a year. But I am not terribly funny. Thus I make almost nothing. If I could think of more jokes like this I would be rich:

> *A guy walks into a bar.*
> *He says to the bartender: "Make me a Bloody Marvin."*
> *"What's a Bloody Marvin?" asks the bartender.*
> *"It's the same as a Bloody Mary," the guy says.*
> *"So why not just order a Bloody Mary?" the bartender asks.*
> *"I'm a feminist," says the guy.*

JASON KUCSMA: What era doesn't need them? Seriously, though, I think it is more crucial than ever for there to be artists and activists telling the stories that aren't being told. With the concentration of mainstream media running rampant, it becomes even more crucial for people to be out there making media and art that challenges the monopolization of what it means to be alive.

When they've tortured and scared you for twenty-odd years then they expect you to pick a career. But you can't really function, you're so full of fear.
—JOHN LENNON

WHAT LIES AHEAD

**(WHAT'S YOUR PROGNOSIS FOR THE FUTURE—
YOURS AND HUMANITY'S?)**

GARY BADDELEY: We're fairly convinced that the ongoing consolidation and concentration of the media will open up plenty of opportunities for alternative voices. When there's hegemony of any kind a new culture always emerges from the underground. There's no doubt that American culture has become very corporate, so it's important for artists and activists to generate an "anti-" culture. We're trying to position Disinformation on the edge between the mainstream and the underground, so that underground voices can be heard by a mainstream (read: large) audience.

SUSANA SANTIZO: I will be fine, spiritually and financially. The world? I have faith in mankind. I believe we will eventually return to our original lifestyles. It will be a long and rough battle and I will never see it or my grandchildren but it will happen. "As it was in the beginning so shall it be in the end."

SANDER HICKS: Prognosis is a nice choice of words. Dictionary.com's defines a prognosis as "A prediction of the probable course and outcome of a disease." You either cure the disease or the patient dies.

GEORGIA GIANNIKOURIS: A few weeks ago, I sat down and typed a list called "What I want to achieve by 30." I can honestly say, that at this point in my life, barely 21, I am preparing to face a very rough road ahead, but it is one that I am approaching headfirst (or heart-first, rather), because I am only settling for the utmost excitement and fulfillment that life has to offer. Here goes:

To be in one play.
To learn Pachelbel's Canon *on my violin (which I have yet to touch).*
To collect all my poems and neatly organize them.
To complete one large painting.
To reach advanced level dance classes.
To write an inspirational book.
To travel to several new countries.
To inspire one person.

Looking at this list now, I'm basically done with number four, and I'm definitely starting number seven. I'm on my way to Australia to study for the upcoming semester, and I've gone to Paris, which I've dreamt of for years. Yet I have always believed that my problem is that I am not focused enough on just one thing. I am totally in love with SO many different things that I am constantly at a war with myself over which to do first.

TIM WISE: My future is good, I hope. I am cautiously optimistic about humanity's. It all depends on us.

GREG RAPAPORT: My prognosis is that there will always be people who go against the grain, that's just part of human nature. They are the ones who push humanity to evolve.

MARTA RUSSELL: Civil rights ignited indignation over issues of exclusion and inequality, but the future calls for a new solutions to ensure the general welfare. We must ignite indignation over the injustice of the few benefiting greatly at the expense of the many. Any worthwhile revolution must be accessible. My goal as a writer has been to expose my "left" readers to the politics of disablement and to expose my disabled readers to the need for radical politics within disability politics. To me radical change means an irreversible change in social relations, human consciousness and in human custom, not simply the imposition of a new administration or a few reformist laws. WE must expand the core of activists that already exist—expand it in such a way that the new activists represent a wider circle of direct acquaintance, a potentially wider ultimate outreach. Mass movements have to expect protracted struggle. "Pessimism of the intellect, optimism of the will"—I think it was Antonio Gramsci, who became disabled while in prison, who said that.

RACHEL MORIELLO: I don't really know that I have a "prognosis" for the future. I'm just going to keep doing what I'm doing and try to make a difference while I'm here.

MICKEY Z.: I wrote a haiku that sums up my prognosis:
i thought i saw a
glimmer of hope but it was
something in my eye

SPARROW: As for the future of the human social race, today I am worried. My wife found the July 2000 issue of *Harpers* magazine, which the Olive Library discarded, and I've been reading the lead article, "Running Dry: What Happens When the World No Longer Has Enough Freshwater?" by Jacques Leslie. "As many as 1.2 billion people—one out of five on the globe—lack access to clean drinking water. Nearly three billion live without sanitation... More than 5 million people a year die of easily preventable waterborne diseases such as diarrhea, dysentery and cholera." And what will we do by 2050, when there are nine billion global people? How can we preserve the lives of so many poor? Perhaps heroes will arise to guide us.

I have no money, no resources, no hopes. I am the happiest man alive."
—HENRY MILLER

Sometimes I wish I were this old guy sitting on the mountaintop subsisting on berries, grasshoppers, or whatever. I wouldn't have to deal with the glazed eyes and lying dullness of my fellows, but I've got to admit I'm a sucker for modern plumbing and the racetrack. Well, I've built my little dungheap and here I sit flinging the shit about. There are minor and major regrets. And it's a hell of a thing to say but—I never met another man I'd rather be. And even if that's a delusion, it's a lucky one.
—CHARLES BUKOWSKI

WOULD YOU LIKE TO SUGGEST ANY RESOURCES?

MANNY SIVERIO: Try some of these:
Director's Guild of America
   http://www.dga.org
Hispanic Organization of Latin Artists (Actors)
   http://hellohola.org/ HOLA
Screen Actors Guild
   http://www.sag.org/
American Federation of Television/Radio Artists
   http://www.aftra.org/
Hollywood Reporter (Trade Magazine)
   http://www.hollywoodreporter.com
Independent Feature Project
   http://www.ifp.org/
   http://www.hollywood.com/
Black Film Maker magazine
   http://www.blackfilmmakermag.com/
Resource site for buying books on film, etc.
   http://www.mwp.com/pages/books.html
   http://www.videomaker.com
My wife Addie's site
   http://www.addie-tude.com

CHAZ MENA: Resources? Epictitus, Marcus Aurelius, Cicero, the Stoics. They have helped me realize that I am responsible only for those things that I can do to help my career along. This advice was given to me, and I would pass it along to others. Film: *Memories of the Underdeveloped* (1973, directed by Tomas Gutierrez Alea), a Cuban film that is a textbook study for all that film had to offer last century. Music: avoid much pop.

SUSANA SANTIZO: *Pedagogy of the Oppressed* by Paulo Freire (Continuum International Publishing Group, 2000)

SANDER HICKS: Yeah, if you can find it, *Threat By Example* is the predecessor to this book. It's edited by Martin Sprouse for Pressure Drop Press and was published in 1990. Amazon had 5 used editions for various prices, from $25 to $151.12 (yikes!) as of 2/4/02. They only printed 1500, once! (Double yikes, there are more punks in the Lower East Side than that alone.) Also, I feel Seth Tobocman's *You Don't Have to Fuck People Over to Survive* (Soft SkullPress, 1999), is a life lessons handbook as much as an art book, and not just because of the moralistic sound of the title.

PAMELA RICE: There's just so much! The best thing for a person to do is to come to the Vegetarian Center (121 E. 27th St., Suite 704, 4-7, M-F). Otherwise, he or she can purchase a copy of *101 Reasons Why I'm a Vegetarian* by Pamela Rice for $2 (postage paid) at VivaVegie Society, PO Box 294, Prince St. Sta., New York, NY 10012.

MICKEY Z.: There's one resource that serves as sort of a clearinghouse for many of the suggestions I'd like to make: WBAI 99.5 FM. It's a classroom on the air and has helped transform my life. Support Pacifica.

MARTA RUSSELL: My suggestions:
ADAPT (American Disabled for Attendant Programs Today)
    http://www.adapt.org/
Disabled in Action (New York)
    http://www.disabledinaction.org/
Bazelon Center for Mental Health Law
    http://www.bazelon.org/who.html
Left Business Observer
    http://www.panix.com/~dhenwood/LBO_home.html

Znet
   http://www.zmag.org
Black Radical Congress
   http://www.blackradicalcongress.com/

RICHARD MILLER: Everybody should read *Fear and Loathing in Las Vegas*, by Hunter S. Thompson (Random House, 1998), *The Illuminatus Trilogy* by R.A.Wilson and R. Shea (Dell Publishing Company Inc., 1988), *The Anarchist Cookbook*, William F. Powell(Barricade Books Incorporated, 1972), and *Steal This Book* by Abbie Hoffman (Four Walls Eight Windows, 2002). There are too many films to recommend, I do after all have a film degree, but I can suggest the following director's work: Jean-Luc Godard, Dario Argento, Alex Cox, George Romero, Peter Jackson, and Lucio Fulci. Most of the work by any of these people will provide plenty to think about, or not to think about. The web is always changing, but www.indymedia.org will probably be around for a while as will www.alternet.org these are both excellent information sources.

JEN ANGEL: *Best of Temp Slave!, Jeff Kelly* (Garrett County Press, 1998)
   Temp Zine! (10364 Davison Rd. #7, Davison, MI, 48423)
   Sabotage in the American Workplace: edited by Martin Sprouse (Pressure Drop Press, 1992)
   For inspiration/how others are leading their lives:
   Threat by Example, edited by Martin Sprouse (Pressure Drop Press, 1990)
   Not For Rent: Conversations with Creative Activists in the UK, Stacey Wakefield & Grrrt (Seattle: Evil Twin Productions, 1995)

SPARROW: Who am I to advise young writers what to read or watch? But I can tell them my most recent personal discoveries:
   Aladdin and Other Favorite Arabian Night Stories, edited by Philip Smith (Dover Children Thrift Editions, 1993)
   My Life in Art by Ludwig Bemelmans (Harper, 1958)

*On the Trail of the Assassins: My Investigation and Prosecution of the
    Murder of President Kennedy* by Jim Garrison (Sheridan Square, 1988)
Antigone by Sophocles (translated by HD F Kitto, (Oxford Press, 1962)
Some like It Hot (1959) Directed by Billy Wilder
42nd Street (1933) Directed by Lloyd Bacon
The Shroud of Turin by Daniel C. Scavone (Greenhaven, San Diego, 1989)
Pogo, Volume 9 by Walt Kelly (Fantagraphics, 1998)
The Story of George Washington Carver by Eva Moore (Scholastic, 1985)
Top Hat (1935) Directed by Mark Sandrich
The Return of Martin Guerre by Natalie Zemon Davis (Harvard University
    Press, 1985)

PANYIOTA PHAROS: A book I read as a child that I will forever hold very dear to
my heart: *There's a Boy in the Girl's Bathroom*, by Louis Sachar (Novel Units
Inc., 1994). Any child I come across I recommend this book for them—even
adults! Sometimes we all feel like monsters in a very big and intimidating world.
If I had enough money I would buy this book for everyone to read—especially
for young, impressionable children who can feel so separated from the rest of
society. I know *I* did and this made me feel like I wasn't the only one out there.

Sometimes I wish I were this old guy sitting on the mountaintop subsisting on berries, grasshoppers, or whatever. I wouldn't have to deal with the glazed eyes and lying dullness of my fellows, but I've got to admit I'm a sucker for modern plumbing and the racetrack. Well, I've built my little dungheap and here I sit flinging the shit about. There are minor and major regrets. And it's a hell of a thing to say but—I never met another man I'd rather be. And even if that's a delusion, it's a lucky one.
—CHARLES BUKOWSKI

CONTACT INFORMATION

JEN ANGEL, *visit:* www.clamormagazine.org

SETH ASHER: sethasher@mindspring.com

GARY BADDELEY, *visit:* www.disinfo.org *or write him at:*

    The Disinformation Company Ltd.

    163 Third Avenue, Suite 108

    New York, NY 10003

RACHEL F.: can be contacted through the publisher.

GEORGIA GIANNIKOURIS: AgapiGG22@aol.com

CHRISTINE HAMM, *visit:* www.dancingartichoke.com

SANDER HICKS: sander@softskull.com or *visit*: www.sanderhicks.com

INDIO (JOHN WASHINGTON): streetnewsbiz@aol.com

RUSS KICK: russ@mindpollen.com

JASON KUCSMA, *visit:* www.clamormagazine.org

CHAZ MENA: chazmena@aol.com

RICHARD MILLER: drachirrel@aol.com

RACHEL MORIELLO: Sugarshock@onebox.com

CHRISTINA MOSES: ubuntuone@aol.com

A.D. NAUMAN: adnauman@aol.com

PANAYIOTA PHAROS: Panayiota1@aol.com

GREG RAPAPORT: www.gregrapaport.com

PAMELA RICE: The Vegetarian Center: 646-424-9595

MARTA RUSSELL: ap888@lafn.org

SUSANA SANTIZO: susanalovei@yahoo.com

MANNY SIVERIO: www.mannysiverio.com

SPARROW (MICHAEL GORELICK): Sparrow44@Juno.com

TIM WISE: tjwise@mindspring.com

MICKEY Z. (MICHAEL ZEZIMA): mzx2@earthlink.net

ORIGINAL QUESTIONNAIRE

Please start with a bio of approximately 300-500 words. If possible, include your year of birth, current place of residence, what it is about you that is "non-main-stream" (i.e. poet, painter, musician, non-consumer, organizer of demonstrations, gay, vegan, atheist, punk, non-motorist, radical, subversive, dissident, revolutionary, etc.), and anything else you feel must be explained. Then, please address the following:

How would you describe your current financial situation? Contrast that with, say, five years ago. What are your expectations in this area over the next few years?

What are some the jobs/money-making ventures you've endured during your time as an artist and/or activist? Feel free to go into extreme detail.

Was there a clear point (dare I say "turning point") when you either decided or simply realized that you were never going to pursue a life and career that would qualify as "normal" by our society's standards? If so, please explain. If not, would you care to comment on that?

Tell me about your first "real" job.

What was the absolute worst job you ever had and why? The best? The biggest "sell-out" job? The most lucrative? The most illegal? Talk about some of your bosses and co-workers.

Any interesting job interview experiences? Best and worst interview questions?

What's the biggest lie on your resume?

What unusual qualifications do you have to offer a potential employer? (feel free to have fun here)

How many times have you been fired? Downsized? Quit?

Have you ever received unemployment insurance or worker's compensation?

Did you ever do 9-to-5? A cubicle? Corporate? Suit and tie or pantsuit? Have you ever had a job that required a uniform (other than suit and tie or pantsuit)? Name tag? Work boots?

Are you ever tempted to "go mainstream"? Are you currently working in a mainstream or corporate environment as a way to stay afloat while pursuing other interests?

If you could be doing what you really want to be doing, what exactly would it be? If you are doing what you want to do, to what do your attribute that "success"?

Has 9/11 affected your art, your income, your activism, your life, etc.?

How has your choice to become an artist and/or activist (or your subsequent status as an outsider) affected any of the following areas?

    Love life
    Sex life
    Family life
    Living situation
    Friends (more? less? how varied?)

THE MURDERING OF MY YEARS

General social life
The way you dress
What you eat (and how often)
Health
Education
Legal issues

Has your choice to become an artist and/or activist caused you to make sacrifices that you sometimes regret?

Who has inspired you and why? (If no one, tell me why).

What tools do you utilize to pursue your passions?

(This can be answered literally or metaphorically.)

Do you have any advice for someone about to embark on a life an artist and/or activist?

Why does twenty-first century America need artists and activists? What is your prognosis for the future (both yours and humanity's)?

Can you suggest any resources for the readers?